I0704398

In the Crucible of Identity

Godfrey Mwakikagile

Copyright © 2020 Godfrey Mwakikagile
All rights reserved.

In the Crucible of Identity

First Edition

ISBN 9798675721689

Kindle Direct Publishing
United States of America

Dedicated to the victims of racial injustice

Introduction

RACIAL IDENTITY and its challenges is the focus of this work. It is based on my personal experience. But it is also a work of universal relevance because of the universal nature of race relations among men and women of all countries as a global phenomenon.

People of all races have their own individual identities. They also have racial identities which unite them with the people who belong to the same race they do. They also share a common identity with other human beings because they are all human. They may have differences with other people but they are all united by common bonds of humanity.

Unfortunately, in many cases, bonds of humanity are fragile. They are even dismissed by some people as irrelevant to our identities as human beings. To them race is paramount even if it means giving it priority at the expense of the well-being of other people.

My identity as a black man has sometimes undergone severe testing, and enormous challenges, from some people who have been unwilling or have simply refused to accept my humanity as a full human being equal to them because of their belief that they are members of a superior race.

They believe that they are better than I am – and better than all black people – in every conceivable way especially in intelligence which, they claim, separates us from the rest of mankind because of our low mental calibre as a product of our poor genetic endowment.

Why God, in His infinite wisdom, would single us out and make us less intelligent than other people when He says – at least according to my belief as a Christian – that He made man in His image is something they have not been able to explain.

We will never know how God thinks let alone understand His eternal existence; such are the inscrutable ways of Providence. Discriminating against some people, in a way only He would understand if He did that, is clearly not one of them.

But it is a harsh reality, this persistent refusal by some people to accept blacks as equal human beings, I as a black man has had to face and contend with, at different times, in my life.

Yet, in spite of all that, I am also aware there are many people of all races who don't believe that black people are less human than other human beings.

Still, racism persists. It is not a rational belief. It is a form of superstition. And it has blinded man to reality, and common sense, since the beginning. And it will continue to exist and ruin the lives of many people till kingdom come. We can only mitigate its effects.

We are all God's chosen people because God chose to make us all. And we all can be saved if we truly repent our sins, however abominable, because of the infinitude of God's mercy.

Dehumanising, hence hating fellow men, and wishing they should *never* have been born and don't even deserve to live because of what they are – black, white or brown – is one of the biggest sins that has caused so much grief, strife and turmoil in the world because of man's immense capacity for evil.

Racial identity is immutable. And we shouldn't wish it to be any other way in spite of the harsh realities some people face in life because of what they are. I have faced my own and will continue to face them in the crucible of my identity without wishing to have been born other than what I am just to escape the ignominy of being despised because of the way God made me in His image.

James Baldwin once said he was born a man to suffer and a nigger to be despised. It is a harsh reality that has tested my patience, and my endurance, but has never broken my spirit.

I have been despised as "a nigger," yet I have prevailed against all odds to be what I am, especially in terms of my moral and spiritual integrity, although I could have done and achieved more in my life than I already have had I not encountered obstacles in pursuit of my goals because of my racial identity which has always been an asset rather than a liability to whites and even to many other nonblacks who are accepted more than blacks are.

None of that has diminished my humanity even when it is denied by others who think they are better than I am and feel better when they insult and ridicule black people. Racial identity has nothing to do with man's intrinsic worth.

In the Crucible of Identity: Challenges of Race

MY LIFE in the United States was never a whirlwind of social interactions across the colour line. I interacted with both worlds, black and white, but mainly with blacks as a member of the black community in which I lived for many years.

It is in my position as a member of that community that I also had lively exchanges with some black Americans – African Americans – who asked me questions about Africa and about my being in the United States including "How do you like it here?"– a common question foreigners from all parts of the world and of all races are asked when they come to this country.

Two of them, both black, even asked me some questions which were loaded with anti-foreign sentiments when I lived in the inner city in Grand Rapids, Michigan. That was in the summer of 1977.

One of them who was a college student from another state, staring at me and shaking his head, said to me point blank: "You guys come over here and just stay. When are you going back to your country?"

The other one, a native of Grand Rapids but who was not a student, asked me: "How many miles is your home country from here?"

I said more than eight thousand miles.

Then he asked me: "Why did you come so far away from home?"

I said I came here to go to school.

"Don't you miss home? It's good to go back."

The implication was that we come all the way from Africa – this applies to other foreigners as well – to deprive them of opportunities, take their jobs, "There aren't enough even for us" is the shared sentiment, and whatever we can take away from them because it does not belong to us.

There is even the accusation that foreigners come to the United States to take their women.

Some men in other countries feel the same way, a sentiment that has been expressed, sometimes with deadly force, by men in South Africa against black African immigrants and in Kenya where Nigerians have been accused of taking women from Kenyans.

In Ghana, as in Kenya, South Africa and other countries, Nigerians are also accused of committing crime and bringing in drugs.

Other African immigrants in South Africa, not just Nigerians, have been victims of xenophobic violence, accused of committing crime, bringing in drugs and even "taking our women."

"Taking our women" is a highly emotional issue among some men in many countries. But it is no more than anti-foreign sentiment.

It is a position that was also articulated by one black American who was my fellow student at Wayne State University in Detroit in 1974. He was a postgraduate student, much older than I was. He said he was 45 when I was 24. He said to me: "You guys like our women, don't you?"

It is rare for American blacks to express such sentiments, or ask such questions, when they are interacting with fellow blacks from other countries. But there are those who do.

Almost invariably, some of the questions Americans ask Africans is: "Where are you from? Did you come here to go to school?" They also sometimes ask why you came to the United States.

Compared with other countries, especially in Africa and other parts of the Third World, Americans know their country is a land of opportunity, including educational opportunities, attracting people from round the globe. Yet many of them still ask basically the same question: "Why did you come here?"

The answer is clear and simple. People come to the United States for different reasons. Yet all those reasons have one common denominator: America is a land of opportunity. It is the land of milk and honey. It is paradise on earth.

Some foreigners want to be American so much that they say they were "born here." They include those who came to the United States as children and can easily get away with that because they don't speak with a foreign accent. They are as American as any other American who was born on American soil – except that they were not born in the United States.

Many Africans come from poverty-stricken or strife-torn countries and see opportunities everywhere in the United States while black Americans don't. Africans see the United States as a land of abundant opportunities – of unlimited possibilities – to succeed in life and will take any job, including jobs blacks Americans don't want to take, as long as they earn some money to live on.

That is the fundamental difference between the two. And it partly explains why black immigrants from Africa and the Caribbean sometimes succeed while American blacks don't under the *same* circumstances in the ghetto, in the *same* country, and with the *same* opportunities *everywhere*.

Sometimes, some black immigrants take *anything* and tolerate *anything* including very low wages and insults from racists to succeed in life while black Americans don't. One of the main reasons they do that is desperation. They are desperate as foreigners in a foreign land.

Many of them also don't want to go back home because life in their home countries is harder, much harder, than it is in the United States even if they earn less than minimum wage. That is why even some of them would rather stay in the United States and work in factories or earn minimum wage even if they have college degrees – including master's and sometimes even PhDs – than go back to their home countries.

As Americans born and brought up in the United States, African Americans expect and *are entitled* to comparable wages whites earn as fellow citizens. They don't expect to be treated as second-class citizens or as strangers in their own land. Contrasted with that is the attitude of many African immigrants who "ain't used to nothing good where they came from." They accept lower wages which are much higher than what they would have earned in their home countries.

It is not because African Americans don't want to work when they don't accept very low-paying jobs earning only "slave" wages – why don't whites also take them, why only blacks and other nonwhites?

Black people in the United States have been some of the hardest-working in the nation's history. They laid the foundation of America. And they have made an enormous contribution to the development and industrialisation of the United States.

Had it not been for the labour of African slaves and their descendants, there would be no United States today as the richest and most powerful country in the history of mankind; it would not even have survived as a nation, especially in its easily days when labour was much needed for it to survive, a reality many whites don't want to face let alone acknowledge.

Whatever benefits and rights African immigrants and

other nonwhites enjoy in the United States have been the result of the relentless struggle and enormous sacrifices American blacks have made through the years to achieve racial equality.

It is a struggle that also has cost countless lives of black people in America for centuries; their pain and suffering immortalised in heart-rending Negro spirituals such as "Nobody Know the Trouble I've Seen," "Sometimes I Fell Like a Motherless Child" and many others, out of more than 6,000 spiritual songs, yearning for freedom.

That has been the struggle for black people in America. And they *still* have not achieved full racial equality.

The refusal by many whites – as well as many other nonblacks – to accept black people as equal human beings and as fellow citizens entitled to the same rights they are, has even led some of them to remember with nostalgia the days when blacks lived under slavery. They are proud of their ancestors who enslaved blacks instead of being ashamed of what they did.

There are also many foreigners who have a low opinion of black Americans and don't even appreciate the sacrifices they made to make America a better country. They include some immigrants, including a number of black immigrants from Africa and the Caribbean, who say black people in the United States don't want to work or they don't work hard enough – all they do is blame the white man for all their problems.

And where do these black immigrants end up when they come to the United States? Mostly in the inner city, in the ghetto, to live with fellow blacks, black Americans, for obvious reasons, people who helped pave the way for them to succeed in America when they waged heroic struggles to achieve racial equality which has helped other nonwhites, including African and Afro-Caribbean immigrants, get opportunities for jobs and education in the United States.

Had it not been for African Americans fighting for their rights, African immigrants and others would not be able to get the opportunities they get when they come to the United States: opportunities for jobs, education, housing and so on. They paved the way for them in a way many black immigrants will never be able to understand and appreciate the sacrifices made by American blacks on their behalf as well, not just for themselves because they were born and brought in the United States and are American citizens.

African immigrants and other blacks who come to the United States in large numbers settle in the inner city more they do anywhere else for different reasons.

The primary reasons are: As blacks, they naturally gravitate towards fellow blacks, African Americans in the ghetto. Also, as blacks, their chances of living elsewhere outside the black homeland, the ghetto, are limited because of racism just as opportunities for black Americans to move out of the ghetto and live elsewhere are limited for the same reason.

Whether, as a foreigner, you came to the United States to go to school, as I did, or just to live and work, you did so because of the abundant opportunities people in other countries don't have and believe America has almost for anybody to succeed in life.

That is true but it is not that simple; and it shouldn't be: Life is a constant struggle even in "the land of milk and honey" – as the United States is also known to be as much as it is known as "paradise on earth" – although many people from poverty-stricken countries think everybody in America is rich or has a lot of money and life is comfortable for everybody who lives here or who comes to this country.

The harsh reality is that America is not paradise on earth.

From Africa to America:
A personal transition

I came to the United States in November 1972.

I remember just before I left, one of my relatives-in-law, Brown Ngwilulupi, married to my mother's first cousin, told me he had just returned from Chicago.

As a high-ranking government official, he travelled outside the country now and then. I went to visit the family and tell them I would be leaving for the United States in a few days. They lived in the nation's capital Dares Salaam where I also lived and worked.

He went on to say that some people think "roads in America are paved with gold. There are poor people in America." He spoke in English when he said that. Most of the time, we spoke in Swahili.

I knew what he said was true. And he probably knew I did as well, since he knew I was a news reporter of Tanzania's largest newspaper, the *Daily News*, formerly the Tanganyika *Standard,* which was also one of the three largest in East Africa, a region comprising three countries: Kenya, Uganda and Tanzania.

Someone in my position would not be that ignorant and believe that all Americans had plenty of money – a lot of it just to give away to the poor in Third World countries, especially those in Africa, paradoxically the richest yet poorest continent.

Still, he said all that probably to emphasise one point: the misconception many people in Tanzania and other parts of Africa and the rest of the Third World have that there is no poverty in America and Americans are awash with money. I was not one of them.

But I knew that the United States, as a highly developed country, had opportunities my home country did not have. That was the main reason I decided to come here – to go to school; which answers the question I was asked by different people at various times through the years why I came to America.

The managing editor of the *Daily News*, Benjamin Mkapa, helped me to come to the Untied States. Years later, he was elected president of Tanzania. He served for for two five-year terms from 1995 to 2005. He died on 23 July 2020.

I left Dar es Salaam on November 3rd and arrived in New York City on November 4th, three days before the American presidential election on November 7th the incumbent, Richard Nixon, won against his Democratic opponent George McGovern in one of the biggest landslide victories in the nation's modern history.

After arriving in New York, I flew to Greensboro, North Carolina, where I intended to attend college. But fate determined otherwise. After being there for only a few days, I left Greensboro aboard a Greyhound bus and returned to New York where I stayed with a relative-in-law, Weidi Ngwilulupi Mwasakafyuka, who was a diplomat at the Tanzania Mission to the UN. He was a younger brother of Brown Ngwilulupi. I stayed in New Yiork for almost two months from November to December.

When I was in New York, I also got the chance to visit Washington, D.C. That was in November. I went there to visit two friends from Trinidad, Anthony (Tony) Ferguson and Wilbur Hilsop, who stayed with me in Dar es Salaam when they came to Tanzania in July-August 1972.

They were Pan-Africanists and political activists interested in forging strong ties between Africa and the African diaspora in a spirit of Pan-African solidarity.

They were also great admirers of President Julius Nyerere of Tanzania as an ardent Pan-Africanist. They also greatly admired Tanzania for the role the country played in the quest for genuine independence and in the Pan-African world as a beacon of hope and strong supporter of the liberation movements in the countries of southern Africa and Guinea-Bissau in West Africa which were still under white minority rule.

The struggle for racial equality in African countries under white minority rulers was intense and bitter and had striking parallels to the struggle for racial equality in the United States during the civil rights movement. But there were also some differences.

The fundamental difference between the two was not in the nature of the struggle but in the methods employed to achieve their common goal of racial equality. The struggle for racial equality by blacks in the United States was fundamentally non-violent. In Africa, freedom fighters resorted to violence. They chose the armed struggle, as the last resort, after the white minority rulers refused to make meaningful concessions to black people on their demands for freedom and equality.

When African leaders met in Addis Ababa, Ethiopia, in May 1963 to form the Organisation of African Unity (OAU), they chose Tanganyika to be the headquarters of all the African liberation movements under the leadership of President Julius Nyerere. The country changed its name to Tanzania when it united with Zanzibar in April 1964 to form the United Republic of Tanganyika and Zanzibar. It was renamed Tanzania in October the same year.

The union was hailed by many people in the Pan-African world, including the diaspora, as a bold move and significant step towards continental unity under one government.

After staying with me in Dar es Salaam, Anthony (Tony) Ferguson and Wilbur Hilsop returned to the United States. I told them I would be in the United States in a few months.

When I went to Washington, D.C., to visit them, I stayed with Anthony Ferguson. I was there for only a few days.

I also met, through them, a Tanzanian, Emmanuel Muganda, who was a fellow student of Anthony at Howard University.

I knew some of Emmanuel's relatives in Dar es Salaam. I worked with his elder brother, Alex Muganda, at the *Standard* newspaper. He worked as a news reporter during holidays when he was a law student at the University of Dar es Salaam. He later joined the Ministry of Foreign Affairs and after a number of years was appointed ambassador to Zimbabwe, among other diplomatic posts.

I also knew their younger sister, Nellie Muganda, who worked as an information officer at the Ministry of Information and Broadcasting where my relative-in-law, James Mwakisyala, a nephew of Brown and Weidi Ngwilulupi Mwasakafyuka, also worked. I also worked there for a few months but after they left.

Emmanuel Muganda also was a journalist. He was, for many years, a news broadcaster in Kiswahili on the Voice of America (VOA) in Washington D.C. and served as head of the Swahili programme at the station.

After visiting Washington, D.C., I returned to New York. Towards the end of December 1972, I left New York for Detroit where I had been given a scholarship by the Pan-African Congress-USA, an African-American organisation, to attend school there.

I graduated from Wayne State University in 1975. In January 1976, I moved to Grand Rapids to attend Aquinas College.

One of my professors of economics at Aquinas College was Kenneth Marin. He worked in Dar es Salaam as an economic adviser to the government when I was still there. But I did not know him. He went to Tanzania in 1968.

Before he went to Tanzania, Professor Marin was a member of the White House Consumer Advisory Council. He was appointed by President Lyndon B. Johnson to serve on Wage and Price Control.

In 1966, Professor Marin was a member of a U.S. State

Department evaluation team that was assigned to review various performances in the economic and political arena in six South American countries.

After he left Tanzania, he returned to his home town, Grand Rapids, to teach at Aquinas College, his alma mater. He was also a graduate of the University of Michigan.

He often talked about the years he spent in Tanzania. One day in an economics class, Professor Marin talked about the place where he worked in Dar es Salaam and about some of the people he worked with. He worked in the Cooperative Building on Lumumba Street.

I told him I had a relative-in-law, Brown Ngwilulupi, who worked in the same building when he was there. He said he knew him and used to have lively exchanges with him on various subjects, especially economic development in Tanzania and Africa in general.

Ngwilulupi was the Secretary-General of the Cooperative Union of Tanganyika (CUT), the largest farmers' union in Tanzania, appointed by President Nyerere.

Years later, Ngwilulupi left Tanzania's ruling party, Chama Cha Mapinduzi (CCM), its Swahili name which means the Party of the Revolution or the Revolutionary Party, and co-founded the country's largest opposition party, Chadema, and served as its vice chairman.

Professor Marin was a great admirer of President Nyerere and described him as "a world leader." He said "He is one of the best world leaders we have today."

He admired Nyerere so much that he even read some of his writings to us in class when he taught economics. But he disagreed with his socialist policies known as Ujamaa in Kiswahili, meaning "familyhood," which was an African version of socialism also known as African socialism.

He also said he and his family went to the same Catholic Church, St. Peter's, President Nyerere did, in Oysterbay, Dar es Salaam.

He said he used to see Nyerere there every Sunday with very little security, only one bodyguard, mingling with other church members just like an ordinary person. Nyerere was known for his humility and very simple lifestyle, unusual for most leaders.

His eldest child, Andrew, was just as humble. We were in school together in Dar es Salaam and stayed in the same hostel. He was just like any other student.

Before I went to Aquinas College, there had been another student from Tanzania, Enos Bukuku, who was also a student of Professor Marin. I was the second student from Tanzania to attend Aquinas College.

Bukuku returned to Tanzania and later taught economics at the University of Dar es Salaam. In the following years, he also served as an economic adviser to President Nyerere. He held other posts at different times. Years later, he became deputy secretary-general of the East African Community (EAC), an economic bloc originally comprising three countries – Kenya, Uganda and Tanzania – and later six, including Rwanda, Burundi, and South Sudan.

Professor Marin talked about Bukuku one day in class, saying he was one of his students and that after he returned to Tanzania he held important positions in the government and was a member of the Tanzanian delegation that went to the People's Republic of China to negotiate with the Chinese leaders for assistance to finance the construction of the Tanzania-Zambia Railway, known by its acronym, TAZARA.

When I first went to Aquinas College, I did not know there was a professor there who once worked in Tanzania and who would be one of my teachers.

I first learned about Professor Marin from my political science professor, Glenn Barkan. I was talking to him in his office one day and when I told him I came from Tanzania, he told me there was an economics professor, Kenneth Marin, who once worked in Tanzania. That is how I met Professor Marin. I went to his office to talk to him.

That, briefly, is the story of my journey from Tanzania to the United States and how I ended up in Grand Rapids. My life in Grand Rapids constitutes a major part this book.

Across the colour line

As an integral part of the black community in Grand Rapids, and in Detroit before then, I had similar experiences in terms of race relations black people have had through the years in the Untied States.

There are some striking parallels in terms of race relations between the United States and colonial Tanganyika when I was growing up there. This is important to understand because race relations is one of the subjects African Americans discuss with Africans and other blacks from the Caribbean – and elsewhere – when they meet in this country.

There are those who have a misconception that Africans don't know much about racism and racial discrimination, and have not suffered racial oppression, because they come from countries which are overwhelmingly black. Therefore they have not lived under white domination. That is not true.

We lived under white domination in Africa. We were colonised. That is what colonialism means: a system of racial domination, oppression and exploitation.

When I came to the united States, I was not surprised black people lived under white domination because I already knew about and I knew, from experience, what it means to be dominated by members of another race.

I have not, directly, had very many encounters with racism through the years I have been in the United States, although indirectly it is something almost all blacks are subjected to, all the time, including its cumulative impact on their lives even if it is not directly experienced and not always perceptible in all areas.

The community in which I lived in Grand Rapids – and even in Detroit – was not an oasis of racial harmony. If such communities exist in the Untied States, they are few, very few, given the prevalence and persistence of racism as a nationwide phenomenon.

I lived and spent most of my time in the inner city in Grand Rapids and did not have many encounters with whites as would have been the case had I lived in a predominantly white area. And when I lived in an integrated area, also for many years, I did not interact with many people, black or white, again minimising chances or precluding the possibility of racial encounters had I mingled with many whites.

That partly explains why I have not been involved in very many racial incidents through the years in a city, and in a predominantly white country, where racism still is a major problem and has a disproportionate impact on black people throughout their lives.

Therefore, like all blacks, I am no stranger to racism, except that I came from a country where racial inequalities and discrimination virtually had official sanction during colonial rule as was the case in the United States, especially in the South during the era of segregation, when such injustices against blacks were sanctioned by law.

There are still incidents of racism I have been involved in which are symptomatic of a larger problem in terms of relations between blacks and whites – incidents of raw-naked racism and others of "milder" forms of racism which may not seem to be racially offensive when contrasted with overt prejudice and hostility.

I will give some examples which have been an integral part of my experience in terms of race relations as a black man in the United States.

In early 1974, during winter, I was with one of my roommates, a fellow African student from Ghana, in

Warren, a suburban area of Detroit where, at a meat shop, they refused to sell us some meat and told us we had to wait until June to see if, even then, it would be available to us. Yet all the white customers who were lined up behind us were served and sold some meat.

In the spring of 1976, returning to Grand Rapids (Aquinas College) from Detroit, one of my schoolmates and I passed through Ann Arbor and stopped at a petrol station to buy some petrol for his car. As my schoolmate was filling the tank, I went inside and asked the manager if I could have the key to the restroom. He said, "No. You can't have the key," shaking his head from side to side and looking at me straight face.

A young white man walked in at the same time and heard the manager refuse to give the key. I walked out, getting ready to go into the car so that I could try to use the restroom elsewhere.

The young white man, who seemed to be a teenager, came out and said to me, "Come on, I'll let you use the restroom after I am done." I waited until he came out. I went in to use the restroom. He waited outside until I was done. After I came out, I thanked him and gave him the key to take it back to the manager who, considering his attitude towards me, probably had a habit of calling black people "niggers."

There are many others of his ilk. And there are friendly ones, yet with the same attitude towards blacks.

What happened to me at the petrol station in Ann Arbor reminded me of life in colonial Tanganyika when we had separate toilets labelled "Africans," "Europeans," and "Asians."

Had there been, at the petrol station, a toilet labelled "Blacks" or "Negroes," as was the case in the segregated South in the United States, I would have used it – without even thinking about going into one labelled "Whites" or "Whites Only." I would have known to do the "right" thing.

But there was none labelled "Negroes" at the petrol station because of racial integration.

Therefore, I had the right to use the only one that was available to members of all races even though the petrol station manager didn't want me to use it because I was black, or just a "nigger." He was angry when I asked for the key and, with that kind of attitude, he probably was the type of person who would call a black person "nigger"; and he probably did that day, called me "nigger," but not in front of me.

In 1976 again, as summer was approaching, two white male students and I were working on campus, Aquinas College, when we saw some insects including some spiders. I was staying on campus during time.

As I took some precaution to avoid contact with the insects, one of the students laughed and said to me: "You come from Africa and you are scared of insects?"

There we were, right on American soil, with some insects, in a country where there are also all kinds of insects and even different kinds of animals. Yet, to that student, it was only in Africa where there are insects, and it was only Africans who were not afraid of insects and animals. The wild kingdom was the exclusive domain of Africa and Africans.

It was the same racial stereotype about black people living in the jungle on a continent where the people share space with animals and insects as if they were family members.

It was also this same student who tried to teach me how to drive during that time. I will never know what went on in his mind. Did he really believe I would be able to learn how to drive since I came from the jungle far removed from civilisation and in an environment where living with wild animals, not civilised human beings, was second nature to us?

Did he see me as just another "nigger" like the ones he is used to seeing all the time in the United States –

whether they are born and brought up in the United States or Africa or any other part of the world including the Caribbean?

He may not have thought or felt that way at all. But the condescending and patronising attitude many whites, including liberals, have towards blacks means it is highly probable even some of the ones you think see blacks as equal to them don't mean it at all. For those who were born and brought up in Africa, it is even worse.

As an African, the perception that Africa is still a jungle is painful. But it is something I expect to hear from some whites.

That is almost exactly what was said to me by a white man when I stayed with him and his family for about three days in the spring of 1974.

I was a student at Wayne State University and went to stay with the family in Bay City, Michigan, under an international students programme – every school has its own, some of them don't have any – intended to help foreign students learn about the American way of life and how Americans live.

It was a family of three; husband, wife, and daughter. Their daughter was about 12 years old.

We were at a dinner table, eating, when the husband said to their daughter: "He comes from Africa. But he's different. He's civilised."

The message was clear. The child, probably having heard stories about "savage" Africans running around in the jungle with nothing on except their natural dress, may have been enlightened when she learned from her father that even in the Dark Continent, there were some Africans who were civilised; on a continent where the people with a dark skin also live in darkness because of the darkness in their minds.

That may have been quite a revelation to her, whereas in the past she probably would have been scared of "savage" Africans. Obviously, her father, having said what he said about me, assured her she was safe even in my presence because I was civilised unlike many of my fellow Africans on the continent who were not.

Civilised African!

I was proof of that. For, there I was, all the way from the jungle, going to school in America, land of the civilised, and in the same classroom with some of the brightest civlised America has ever produced.

Yet, to the father, that was a perfectly innocent remark when he introduced me to their child saying, "he's civilised."

Even some whites who socialise with blacks and have black friends or so-called friends who are black, sometimes use the term "nigger," casually, to address or describe black people including their friends. The assumption that calling black friends "niggers" is no more than an expression of genuine camaraderie and the term "nigger" is no more than a casual remark and a term of endearment exposes their true feelings about blacks.

They know what the term "nigger" means. They know that no self-respecting black person likes to be called a "nigger" – there is nothing casual or friendly about it. At a deeper level, it shows how racism has distorted, permeated and corrupted the minds of even some of the most enlightened whites.

I remember one white student, among a few others, who used to come to the house in which I lived with other students in Grand Rapids, casually using the term "nigger" one day in the summer of 1977. I had been in the United States for about four-and-a-half years.

The other students I lived with, all black, went to the same school he did. Some of them were his classmates. There was only one roommate among us, also black, who was not a student.

Three of us, including the white student, were sitting on the porch one afternoon when I got up to go and get or do something in the house. As I was walking into the house, I heard him talking to the other student, who was an African American, telling him so-and-so "is a good nigger." He said my name, in a low tone, but I heard him.

When I came out of the house, he had already left. The black student said to me, so-and-so "said you are a good nigger." I said I heard him.

To that young white man, it was a compliment to call me "a good nigger." To me, as black man, it was an insult. It was no more a compliment calling me a "nigger" than it would have been had he called me "boy" as some whites still do to address and insult full-grown black men.

Yet he was one of the most friendly with blacks and came to our house many times. He came every week, two to three times, and even called us "brothers" – "hey, brother" and so on.

After I moved out in the same year and rented a house with a few other students on a different street not far from my previous residence, he came to visit me. We didn't even know each other very well. I met him for the first time when he came to visit his fellow students at the other house and we had known each other for only a few months. But he wanted to stay in touch with me.

When he went to Europe in the summer of 1977, he even wrote me from there. When I received a letter from one of the West European countries where he spent the summer, I did not have the slightest idea who wrote me when I saw the name of the country where the letter came from. I did not known anyone in that country and I had not given my new address to anybody. Then I found out the letter came from him, after I opened it, and he was looking forward to seeing me again when he returned to Grand Rapids.

His use of the term "nigger" as if it were a compliment or just another word meaning "a black person" years later reminded me of what Mark Fuhrman, the white police officer who investigated O. J. Simpson for the murder of his wife, said when he tried to explain what the term "nigger" meant. He was on the Oprah Winfrey Show one day and she asked him if he didn't think calling a black person "a nigger" was an insult. He said, no, it was not an insult – "nigger" simply meant "a black person."

He had used the term "nigger" many times in his career as a police officer and was emphatic in his response during the interview stating explicitly that to him calling a black person "nigger" was the same as calling him or her "black."

It is not a term that requires nuanced understanding. The context itself, of troubling race relations in the United States, is enough to show that the term means exactly what it means. It has no justification, regardless of the context in which it is used, when whites and other nonblacks, use it to identify or describe black people.

Even calling blacks "Negroes" can be an insult. I have had that experience.

I was involved in a racial incident which had to do with a car accident. That was in 1977.

An African American student and I were involved in the accident. He was the same student who was with me in the same year, 1977, when I was involved in a racial incident with a white student who was also his classmate and who called me "a good nigger."

He was driving when he hit a car driven by a young white woman. There was another woman in the car with her. She was also white. Both seemed to be in their twenties like us.

After only a few minutes, two police officers, both white, came to the scene of the accident. The two white women were already out of their car. We also got out of ours.

One of the police officers asked what happened. The woman who was driving pointed at us and said:

"It is these two Negroes who caused the accident."

The other woman agreed with her. Both were very loud and very angry.

It was the use of the word "Negroes" – at a time when it was no longer used to identify black people as much as it used to be in the past – and the way the driver pointed at us, shaking her finger, which exposed her racist attitude towards us.

The other woman was just as bad, agreeing with everything the driver was saying. And she was just as talkative.

The term "Negro" had been replaced by "black" to describe and identify black people even before then and the two white women knew it was not used for that purpose anymore – not on television, not on the radio, not in the newspapers, not in conversation. They could not have missed that.

The driver of the car was being deliberately provocative and insulting when she called us "Negroes," and with an emphasis, "It is these two Negroes" who were responsible for what happened.

Any white person who calls a black person "Negro," and with such anger, also probably uses the term "nigger" and may even see the use of the term "Negro" as being equivalent to calling a black person "nigger" only in mild form.

The harsh reality is that black people, who are American citizens and are as American as any other American and have been American since and even before there was America as a nation, are not recognised by many whites as Americans or as full citizens. And they are not second-class citizens even if they are treated that way by some whites or by society in general.

Many blacks are painfully aware of that, a recognition of this painful and cruel rejection by some of their fellow countrymen, which prompts some of them to say, "We're just here," meaning they are not recognised or fully accepted as equal citizens. I have heard the expression used a number of times by some blacks, especially by black men, whom I have known for years; a painful reminder that they are strangers in their own homeland.

The resurgence of racism in its overt and virulent form under Donald Trump who was an embodiment of white supremacy – he himself expressed overtly racist views during his presidency – was a clear demonstration of the stubborn refusal by many whites to accept black people as fellow Americans who were not only entitled to equal rights but to respect as fellow human beings.

The malignancy of racism is manifested in many ways – such as brutal mistreatment of blacks, including murder – with black people being the primary target more than members of any other racial or ethnic group; in recent times best exemplified by the horrific death of George Floyd in Minneapolis, Minnesota, on 25 May 2020 at the hands of a racist police officer, Derek Chauvin, who brutally and slowly squeezed life out of him when he dug his knee into Floyd's neck, pressing hard for almost eight minutes as his victim pleaded with him and desperately begged for his life, repeatedly, saying, "Please, please, please, I can't breathe, please....I can't breathe."

A 17-year-old black girl, Darnella Frazier, videotaped the brutal execution. There were several other witnesses. They pleaded with the police officer to stop torturing Floyd and get off his neck. The white police officer who killed him did not even care he was being videotaped. He saw Darnella filming him. Other police officers on the scene also knew they all were being filmed.

Chauvin also knew video cameras on police cars were on and he was being videotaped as required by law. He still didn't care. He knew he was killing Floyd and he believed he could get away with murder because he was a white police officer and the victim was black. Another video camera in the area also captured the brutal slaying.

The brutal execution of George Floyd was a demonstration of white power in its crudest form. The racist policeman was an embodiment, and a symbol, of white supremacy. He symbolised what many whites felt and feel about black people. Their lives mean nothing, absolutely nothing.

What Derek Chauvin did to George Floyd was an expression of a collective sentiment harboured by many whites when a black person is killed by racist police officers or by any white racist – or by anybody else – and even when he or she just dies for whatever reason. The attitude is: "Just another nigger dead. Nothing to worry about."

The attitude of racist police officers across the country was best expressed in an interview Black Panther Party leader Huey P. Newton had on *CBS News Nightwatch* in the 1980s.

He was interviewed by the host, Charlie Rose, and talked about the problems he and his fellow Black Panthers and other blacks had with the police in Oakland, California, where the Black Panther Party for Self-Defense was co-founded by him and Bobby Seale on 15 October 1966 when they were students at Merritt College in that city.

Huey P. Newton told Charlie Rose that the Oakland Police Department was very racist and the bosses there said they liked recruiting police officers from Georgia, a southern state notorious for mistreating blacks like the other southern states. The officers said they were recruited "because we know how to handle niggers."

When blacks are killed by white police officers, there are even many whites who celebrate that: "Good job." And the killing of black people, singled out and targeted just because they are black, has not stopped.

How many of them have to die? And to those who want to make America white again, when was America just white? And when did whites lose power as the dominant race in America?

White people who don't like blacks have to face the

fact, immutable fact and harsh reality, that black people are going nowhere. As Dr. Martin Luther said, "We are in America, we are here to stay, we ain't going *nowhere*."

Black people are not "going back to Africa." The United States is their country and it will always be.

White people have to learn, whether they like it or not, to accept black people not only as fellow Americans but as fellow citizens entitled to the same rights they are entitled to – unless they are prepared to live in a society that will become unstable until its black citizens are accorded full citizenship rights in the practical sense, not just in the legal sense on paper.

Racism makes that impossible. And it is the main complaint you hear from blacks, although some of them use it to justify their failure and unwillingness to help themselves even without trying.

I have heard of cases like that. One was extreme.

In 1978, I heard a young black man, whom I only knew casually and who was close to my age and was working, say, "I'm quitting – I ain't kidding. I'm applying for welfare. All I have to say is they called me 'nigger' at work." Meaning – that made it impossible for him to continue working there.

"That's how black people. They don't want to work," is the response you hear from some whites.

I also knew a black woman who was also close to my age and who had three children with three different fathers who said something that equally "justified" stereotypes about blacks. She said to me: "I'm lazy. I don't want to work. And with three children – I get a bigger check on welfare than I would if I worked out there."

"What else is new? Typical of blacks in the ghetto," many whites say.

There are such people. But they are a very small minority in the black community, considering the fact that most blacks work.

Yet, they tarnish the image of all blacks, especially in

the ghetto, who are already portrayed by the larger society as irresponsible people who don't want to work, don't want to go to school, don't want to do anything to help themselves – despite overwhelming evidence to the contrary.

Most blacks are not on welfare, living on handouts from the government. And even some of those who don't work and live on government assistance for a long time do so because they can't get jobs due to racism.

Yet, there are also those who take advantage of the system and just don't want to work because assistance is available to them from the government.

There are such people in all racial groups. Yet, blacks are portrayed as being the worst because of racism – blaming them for almost everything that goes wrong in the society – even though there may be some truth to the allegation in some cases in which documented evidence shows, in terms of percentage, that there more blacks than whites on welfare.

But even in such cases, racism cannot be entirely ruled as an explanation, or as a part of the explanation, why the percentage of blacks on welfare is higher than the percentage of whites who are also on welfare.

In terms of sheer numbers, there are more whites than blacks getting assistance from the government. But racism has a way of obscuring and distorting reality in this case as well – it is blacks who are said to be on welfare in far larger numbers than whites.

That is also the case with crime, with blacks being accused of "committing all that crime," a racist and hyperbolic statement. Only a very small percentage of blacks commit crime, sharply contrasted with those who don't.

Grand Rapids is a good example. It is the second-largest city in Michigan after Detroit, yet the crime rate in the inner city, which is the ghetto on the southeast side and overwhelmingly black, is low in spite of the fact that the city has a significant black population in terms of both percentage and numbers.

There is crime in the inner city and other parts of Grand Rapids – no question about that. I was a victim myself, twice, in 1982 when I lived in the inner city.

I was robbed by two black men who were at least in their thirties and they physically attacked me. It was a traumatic experience.

I was able to get the licence plate number of their car and gave it to the police but they were never arrested. The detectives said they could not find them. They were told by their family members they left town. Almost forty years later, I still remember the licence plate number of their car and what kind of car it was.

Two other blacks, teenagers, tried to break into my apartment in the same year. I was in the apartment that night and surprised them when they were trying to break in. I knew them and they were arrested. One of them, who was at least 18 years old, was sentenced to a jail term; the other one, under 15, was not but was placed under parental supervision and the watchful eye of the authorities.

The detective who handled my case came to my residence and asked me to go with him in his car and show him where the teenagers lived. I did. Years later, he became Grand Rapids police chief.

Still, Grand Rapids, the inner city, does not have the reputation other cities have for high crime rates.

And in all those cities, it is not just blacks who commit crime even though the crime rate is often higher in the inner cities than it is other parts. Yet the perception persists among many whites that it is "blacks who commit *all that* crime."

Two white women I knew in Grand Rapids shared that perception. That was in 1980.

We were sharing a table one day when one of them who was old enough to be my mother started talking about crime. It had to do with what I had in my hands. I was reading a newspaper, the *Detroit Free Press*, which I bought quite often although I lived in Grand Rapids and also read *The Grand Rapids Press* even more.

She saw the name of the paper on the front page when I held it up, reading it, and said, "There is a lot of crime in Detroit. It's very dangerous. I don't see how people can live there."

I said to her I used to live tin Detroit, a predominantly black city and one of the largest in the country. It was the fifth-largest when I lived there from the early to the mid-seventies – and it still was for many years – with New York being the largest, followed by Chicago, Los Angeles, Philadelphia, and then Detroit.

What she implied, in coded language used by many racists, was that because the city was mostly black, it was not a safe place to live since blacks "commit all that crime."

The younger white woman, who said she was 20, agreed with her, nodding, and then said: Mhh! It is true. Blacks commit more crime. The FBI says so."

The conversation, even if there were some elements of truth about the high crime rates in large cities and in ghettoes across the nation, highlighted differences in perceptions blacks and whites have about each other.

My experience in America as a black man has been an integral part of the black American experience in contemporary times and during the past several decades since the early seventies, my early years in the United States. It is an experience that has been good and bad, including encounters with racism, some of which have tested my patience.

One such incident took place in 1978. I knew a white man who had a habit of calling blacks "niggers" at a place where one of my African American friends worked. I even heard him call me "nigger," as did another white man who also worked there. He heard him calling us "niggers."

I was 28 years old. He said he was 35. At his age, he

belonged to a generation of whites who usually did not use old terms such as "Negro" and "coloured" to describe black Americans; also in an era when even the majority of Americans of all ages, and all races, no longer used those terms.

One day, calling my name, he said to me: "I watched this movie last night; it was full of coloured folks – all of them *dumb!*"

The implication was obvious. He knew I knew exactly what he meant.

Since when have we, blacks, been considered to be intelligent like other people or as intelligent as anybody else?

The language he used was highly offensive to me as a black man. Besides implying all blacks without exception – not just those in the movie he claimed he saw, if he did at all – were stupid, he also deliberately used the term "coloured folks" to disparage black people.

It was the same white man who asked me one day to go deer hunting with him. He said, "Let's go deer hunting up north." He meant the northern part of Michigan where many hunters go during the deer hunting season.

I knew it was a trap. People have been killed that way by their enemies. When they go deer hunting with them, they are the ones who become prime target, shot as deer, by those who want to kill them for whatever reason.

I brought up the subject in a conversation with one black man who also knew the white racist who asked me to go and hunt deer with him. When I told him I had been invited by that man to go deer hunting with him, he laughed and said: "It's a setup. He's going to shoot you."

I told him I knew it was setup and I was not going to fall into that trap.

But because of the way many whites see us, as stupid and ignorant people without any common sense, the white man thought I trusted him and believed all he was going to do was hunt deer, not me.

Racial stereotypes abound. And they reinforce some of the most racist beliefs white people have about blacks. Some of those stereotypes have to do with sports. I was a victim of that as well in 1978.

The incident involved a young white man who was a foreman at a company where my African American friend I mentioned earlier worked. He also knew me well and was in his twenties, close to my age. He first asked my friend and then asked me one Friday evening: "Let's play basketball this weekend."

I told him, "I don't play basketball."

He couldn't believe what I said. "You are black, and you don't play basketball? Don't make laugh."

He felt out laughing. He thought it was funny to hear a black man say he doesn't play basketball. He just didn't believe me.

Prevalent among many whites is the belief that blacks excel in sports – basketball, boxing, sprinting – for biological or anatomical reasons. It is a part of their nature. They are just made that way. They are nimble and agile. They run very fast and jump very high like monkeys. They are naturally stronger than whites – their brute strength enabling them to win almost all boxing matches, and so on, attributed to their beastly nature, not just training.

It is a subject that has been addressed eloquently by Professor Harry Edwards, an African American, at the University of California-Berkeley, through the years.

There are more stereotypes about blacks: They also can sing and dance very well.

But they cannot do anything cerebral because of their low mental calibre. It's not their fault. They are born that way. They are not well-endowed like whites whose mental faculties are beyond question in terms of excellence.

Even black professors are not considered to be as good as their white counterparts just because they are black. And they are denied tenure, not because they are not qualified but because they are black.

It is a nationwide problem in all academic institutions across the United States which have black faculty members. Here are a few cases of this disturbing phenomenon at Florida International University (FIU). As Teresa Schuster stated in her article, "Discrimination, Microaggressions, and Unfair Treatment: FIU Professors Explain What's Like To Be Black in Academia," *PantherNow*, 6 July 2020:

"Amidst protests for racial justice, Black faculty members have taken to Twitter, using #BlackInTheIvory to share stories of racial bias in universities around the world.

FIU is no exception.

'I think [the movement] is necessary during this time, and can depict what it is like to be a Black faculty member on a day-to-day basis,' said Isaac Burt, an associate professor in FIU's Counseling, Recreation, and Social Psychology department. 'It sheds light on something a number of people may have ignored in the past.'

Academia is purportedly a meritocracy, but the way meritorious is defined is problematic, Burt said.

'Sometimes, as terrible as it sounds, people simplify 'being meritorious' and unconsciously link it to how a person looks,' he said. 'These conscious and unconscious decisions amalgamate, and then a person, regardless of their efforts, is deemed 'unworthy' for recognition, promotion, or tenure.'

Burt says he's experienced some of this himself.

'I have had instances of white faculty commenting on my 'appearance,' insinuating that I do not belong here,' he said.

Black faculty are often made to feel they don't belong, according to Antoinette Smith, an FIU accounting professor.

'If you google 'professor', a white male is going to

come up, [or] a white female is going to come up,' Smith said. 'Someone who doesn't look like us.'

This mentality can spread to everyone on a university campus, and frequently extends to the classroom, said Smith.

'[Students] feel entitled to treat you inhuman[ly],' she said. 'I don't really have a better way of saying that.'

They feel entitled to challenge Black professors' authority, and submit complaints about them more frequently, said Smith. The professors are forced to compensate by overemphasizing their credentials and accomplishments.

'We should not have to prove our worth,' Smith stated.

Some of the animosity towards Black professors is due to their manner of teaching, according to her.

'We come from a history of being excluded from history books, and also of people not telling the whole truth [about] us, so we tend to have a different teaching style,' said Smith, explaining that Black professors often encourage students to do their own research apart from textbooks, which can be seen as unconventional.

'Professors of color have all seen the phrase 'I didn't learn anything' from a student when we know that we have mastered the material and delivered it exceptionally well,' she said.

While Smith encounters less bias from students now, as a more senior professor, she says it remains common.

'It happens to all of us,' she said.

It's especially harmful to Black professors since student evaluations play a role in tenure and promotion decisions, Smith pointed out.

Complaints can determine a professor's future.

'The wrong step, phrase, or look could end your career,' said Smith.

Sheryl Weir-Latty, an instructor at FIU, agrees, saying instructors' security is 'so heavily weighted on the words of students.'

'My position is temporary and I can be fired at any time,' said Weir-Latty, who teaches marketing. 'There are two of us in [my] department of African descent. We're both visiting [instructors]. We fear that a student could say something, and we are no longer able to do what we love to do.'

Weir-Latty believes there should be mechanisms to identify racial bias in student evaluations and complaints.

'There needs to be something in place that really examines the foundation of a student's remarks when they're complaining,' said Weir-Latty. 'Is it a valid statement?'

Taking the bias against Black faculty into account when using student evaluations should be required, according to Smith.

'Executive administrators must be able to consider all factors when evaluating professors of color,' she said.

'What's the demographics of the classroom? Do students in this field typically encounter a professor of color? Did the executive administrator ask the professor about racial biases?' – (Teresa Schuster, "Discrimination, Microaggressions, and Unfair Treatment: FIU Professors Explain What's Like To Be Black in Academia," *PantherNow*, 6 July 2020).

Problems black faculty members face are not confined to the classroom.

Together with black students, black professors find themselves in a hostile environment or around people who don't care about them and even ignore their presence on campus as if they didn't exist at all.

One of the biggest problems they face is that their white colleagues – even other nonblacks – don't see blacks as their equal, intellectually and even socially.

Compounding the problem is the larger society which sanctions such behaviour and conduct and validates racial stereotypes about black people.

It is "us versus them," with blacks collectively being the target as a group of people who don't belong there – they just don't:

"Black faculty face more difficulties beyond the classroom.

Burt says a 'mob mentality' can form in departments, hindering black faculty from achieving tenure and pursuing their research interests.

'Excessively criticizing a Black faculty [member's] work in a prestigious journal, but applauding a white colleague's research in the same journal with minimal judgment or critique,' he explained.

Some faculty do not consider researching race, bias, or discrimination 'truly scholastic endeavors,' according to Burt, and look down on it 'especially if a person of color is the researcher conducting those studies.'

Weir-Latty remembers a Black professor whose department refused to grant him tenure although he 'met and surpassed' the criteria.

After he appealed to FIU's provost, Weir-Latty said they granted it to him.

'But just imagine working in that position where you know that everyone you're going to work with now was against your tenure,' she said.

Being a Black professor at FIU is 'somewhat difficult,' according to Burt.

'I have experienced being completely invisible to my colleagues, but simultaneously hyper-visible,' he said, recalling FIU's annual Martin Luther King Breakfast.

'A previous administrator never spoke to me except for when they asked me to attend the breakfast and sit at their table during the ceremony. At the time, there was only one other Black faculty member, whom they also ignored but asked them to attend as well,' said Burt. 'After two years and recognizing the pattern, I politely declined their offer to attend.'

Burt says the environment in his department has been unrewarding, he's experienced 'numerous cases of microaggressions, unfair treatment, and discrimination,' and seen it done to others.

'An example is intentionally keeping information hidden from Black faculty, then blaming them for not knowing it when they ask,' he said.

Meetings are sometimes toxic as well, according to Weir-Latty, and some professors look down on Black faculty members.

'If you don't view them as your intellectual equal, or knowing just as much as you do, you'll see them and their input as unimportant,' Weir-Latty said.

FIU offers ways to report instances of bias, but according to FIU's Title IX coordinator, Shirlyon McWhorter, cases are 'not always easy to prove' although the implicit bias is prevalent.

'We can see it in hiring and firing decisions that we make every day in terms of promotions and things like that,' said McWhorter....

'Be willing to say something if you see something,' McWhorter said. 'If I'm an African American student and I'm sitting in class and I raise my hand and I never get chosen, [and the professor] always calls on the non-Black students, that shows up as maybe unconscious bias he's not even aware of.'

This harms everyone involved, according to McWhorter.

'[It] impacts the students heavily, which is why it's so important for FIU to work and make sure that we have more professors of color in the classroom,' she said.

Weir-Latty agrees that this is important.

She says a Black student of hers was inspired to become a professor herself, after seeing Weir-Latty in that role.

'If you don't see a person [like you] in a job position, you're going to choose another path,' she said.

Black professors are viewed as less capable, one reason why they aren't hired as much, according to Vanessa Vieites, a psychology Ph.D. student at FIU.

'Biases have been shown to affect employers' hiring decisions, even when given fake but identical resumes,' said Vieites. 'Black and Latinx PhDs, especially those who are women, tend to be viewed as less competent or hireable than comparable white or Asian PhDs'....

'The problem is not just with FIU, but with academia, which includes all the institutions in the nation'....

'We haven't gotten to the point where we find a cure or remedy yet, but we're fact-finding,' said El Paginer K. Hudson, FIU's vice president for human resources, pointing out that FIU tenured 25 faculty at its last Board of Trustees meeting.

'Not one of them was Black,' Hudson said."

Black professors, including some of the most distinguished in their fields, who have made legitimate complaints about racism have sometimes been viciously attacked, vilified and threatened by their colleagues – and even by some white students – in order to silence them.

One of these tragic cases involved George Yancy, a professor of philosophy at Emory University in Atlanta, Georgia, a highly acclaimed scholar in his field who also earned a number of awards – including highest honours – in his field for academic excellence.

Yet some of his white colleagues and students did not acknowledge him as a reputable scholar and insulted him in a vicious way, belittling him, in spite of his accomplishments. As he stated in an article, "The Ugly Truth of Being a Black Professor in America":

"'Dear Nigger Professor.'
That was the beginning of a message that was sent to me. There is nothing to be cherished here, despite the salutation.

Years ago, Malcolm X asked, 'What does a white man call a black man with a Ph.D.?' He answered: 'A nigger with a Ph.D.'

The message came in response to an op-ed I published in *The New York Times* in December 2015.

I'd spent much of that year conducting a series of interviews with philosophers about race. I wanted to hold a disagreeable mirror up to white readers and ask that they take a long, hard look without fleeing.

My article, 'Dear White America,' took the form of a letter asking readers to accept the truth of what it means to be white in a society created for white people. I asked them to tarry with the ways in which they perpetuate a racist society, the ways in which they are racist. In return, I asked for understanding and even love — love in the sense that James Baldwin used the term: 'Love takes off the masks that we fear we cannot live without and know we cannot live within.'

Instead, I received hundreds of emails, phone messages, and letters, an overwhelming number of which were filled with racist vitriol.

My university did its important and necessary part — top administrators assured me that my academic freedom was protected. Yet my predicament was not easy. Campus police had to monitor my office. Departmental instructions were clear: No one was to provide any strangers with my office hours. I needed police presence at my invited talks at other universities. It all felt surreal — and dangerous.

This is what it's like to be the target of racist hatred:

'Another uppity Nigger. Calling a Nigger a professor is like calling White Black and Wet Dry.'

'Even the most sophisticated nigger will revert back to their jungle bunny behavior when excited.'

'You can dress a Nigger up in a suit and tie and they'll

still be Niggers.'

'This belief that niggers even reason is blatant pseudo-intellectualism.'

For these writers, 'nigger professor' is an oxymoron. A nigger is a nigger, incapable of reason. Kant, Hegel, and Jefferson each made similar claims about black people being bereft of rationality. Perhaps I'm just parroting (as Hume said of black people) what I've already heard. I'm just a nigger who dared to reason, only to discover that reason is white.

'The concept of there being an intellectual Negro is a joke.'

Perhaps this person had spoken to the woman who left the following on my university answering machine:

'Dear professor, I am a white American citizen. You are the one who is the racist against white people, evidently. A professor — I bet you got it [your PhD] through a mail order.'

On a white racist website, one writer has apparently seen through my game:

'This coon is a philosopher in the same way Martin King was a PHD and the same way that Jesse Jackson and Al Sharpton are 'Reverends': Just another jive assed nigger with a new way to pimp.'

Some of my students of color have asked me, 'Why talk about race with white people when at the end of the day everything remains the same — that is, their racism continues?' 'Why teach courses on race and whiteness?' 'Do you really think that such courses will make a difference?'

I find these questions haunting; they nag at my conscience.

Indeed, there are times when I ask myself, 'Why do I do this?' After all, I don't write about whiteness because it is a new fad in philosophy. And I'm certainly not a masochist. There is no pleasure to be had in being the object of hatred. I'm sure that a few of my black colleagues and colleagues of color think that I've lost my sanity. Perhaps they think that I've asked for all of this and that had I remained silent I would have been fine.

The reality, of course, is that they too are seen as niggers. Silence will not help." – (George Yancy, "The Ugly Truth of Being a Black Professor in America," Blog of the APA (American Philosophical Association), 22 May 2018; originally published in *The Chronicle of Higher Education*).

Besides more insults being heaped on him, his quest for racial reconciliation which took him through the minefields of hate also took terrifying turn:

"In 2015, I was invited to be a plenary speaker at a well-established philosophy conference. I was excited. After all, I was there to deliver my talk within the company of kindred philosophical spirits, those who knew something about feminism, disability, aesthetics, and race. There was one other black philosopher in attendance, though he was older, taller, heavier, and very gray. All the other attendees were white.

The day after I gave my talk, the other black philosopher told me that several attendees had, with no apparent hesitation, complimented him on my talk: 'That was a very important talk that you gave yesterday.' 'Wow, great talk!' 'Inspiring.'

No less than seven congratulatory gestures were made.

Had there been only one or two, perhaps it could have

been brushed off. But seven times?

This was the manifestation of an all-too-familiar mode of being white — a habit of perception that sees black people as all the same, through a fixed imago. This was white racism. My colleague, the black philosopher who had not given the talk, somehow 'became' me, and I him.

In that sophisticated and philosophically progressive white space, I could hear a strange and profoundly irritating echo of the little white child whom Frantz Fanon encountered on a train: 'Look, a Negro!'

There was a familiar sense of being fixed, static. The two of us became one black man; any black man; every black man. We were flattened, rendered one-dimensional, indistinct and repeatable.

'Hey Georgie boy. You're the fucking racist, asshole. You wouldn't have a job if it wasn't for affirmative action. Somebody needs to put a boot up your ass and knock your fucking head off your shoulders you stupid fucking goddamn racist son of a bitch. You fucking race baiting son of bitches. Man, you're just asking to get your fucking asses kicked. You need your fucking asses kicked. You stupid motherfucker. Quit fucking race baiting, asshole.'

It is probably true that I would not have my job were it not for affirmative action. Many white women wouldn't have jobs either! And of course, white men have benefited from white supremacy for years.

But affirmative action is not white supremacy in reverse; it is not antiwhite, but pro-justice. It was created so that with my Ph.D., which I earned with distinction, I would actually be able to teach at a university. Affirmative action, in the case of black people, is a response to systemic racist disadvantages. It's important to get that history right — not twisted.

I felt particularly sickened by the letters — there were quite a few — sent to me through regular postal mail, handwritten and signed. These are even more disturbing than emails, given the level of industry expended (writing, printing, stamping, mailing).

The opening of one such letter read, 'I'm a racist? How dare you call me that! You are a racist and, hey, since blacks call each other 'nigga' I'm taking the liberty of doing the same. Either the word is offensive and taboo or it isn't.'

I'm not buying it. I once had two white male students attempt to argue that they should be allowed to use the word (with the "-er") whenever they wanted, and that it is discriminatory to say that they can't.

Any response at all felt too generous. I have often heard white people express the feeling of being somehow left out from black spaces, which are necessary for black sanity precisely because of white racism.

It is as if white people are driven by a colonial desire to possess everything. Du Bois asked, 'But what on earth is whiteness that one should so desire it?' He answered, 'Whiteness is the ownership of the earth forever and ever, Amen!'

These two white students spoke with arrogance and the desire for total white ownership. It was not so much that they were deprived of historical knowledge, as that rather, this knowledge meant nothing when it came to their sense of loss of power....

One might think that being called a nigger so many times might decrease its impact. It doesn't.

'All black people in the United States, irrespective of their class status or politics,' according to bell hooks, 'live with the possibility that they will be terrorized by whiteness.'

The many responses of white people to 'Dear White America' were just that — 21st-century white terror.

That terror can come in many forms. Perhaps a black man screams 'I can't breathe!' 11 times, but no one cares (Eric Garner). Or perhaps, after he has been shot by 'accident,' he musters enough strength to say aloud that he's losing his breath (Eric Harris), only to hear a white police officer respond, 'Fuck your breath!'

Perhaps his spine gets severed (Freddie Gray). Perhaps he is a teenager and is shot 16 times (Laquan McDonald). Pulling out a wallet can lead to getting shot at 41 times and hit with 19 bullets (Amadou Diallo). Perhaps an innocent 7-year-old black child (Aiyana Stanley-Jones) is killed by police during a raid. Just as was true for Emmett Till 63 years ago, there is no place that one can call safe in America for black bodies....

On November 11, 2017, I received a letter in my university mailbox. It was handwritten on both sides in black ink on a sheet of paper torn from a yellow legal pad. There was no return address. Every time I've touched it, as I must do now for purposes of transcribing it word-for-word, I wash my hands afterward.

'Dear Mr. Yancy, I am writing to you to voice my displeasure with what you said about WHITE PEOPLE.

You claim that all White people are Racists! Really now? You, sir are one to talk!!

You sound just like the following Racists.

Here is a list of who I mean. They're Al Sharpton, Oprah Winfrey, Whoopi Goldberg, Spike Lee, Samuel L. Jackson, Bill Cosby, Danny Glover, Harry Belafonte, Movie Director John Singleton, Shannon Sharpe, Scottie Pippen (former NBA player), Rappers Ice Cube, Chuck D., Flavor Flav, DMX, and Snoop Dogg; former MLB players Carl Everett, Ray Durham and Hall of Famer Hank Aaron!

When I read what you said about White people, I was like this guy is a total lowlife Racist piece of shit! It's so true!

You are an asshole! You deserve to be punished with several fists to your face! You're nothing but a troublemaker! You need to really 'Get a life!' I've had enough of your Racist talk! You'd better watch what you say and to whom you say it! You may just end up in the hospital with several injuries or maybe on a cold slab in the local morgue!

I wouldn't be surprised if you've gotten several Death Threats! You're inviting trouble when you accuse the entire White Race of being Racists! You've got a big mouth that needs to be slammed shut permanently!

I'm not going to give you the opportunity to find out who I am. Good luck with that!

By the way, this letter I'm sending you is certainly not a Death Threat! I could've done that, but that's not me! I'm tired of your Racist kind!'

Please tarry with these words. My life has just been threatened. The writer belies their intention by denying that the letter is a death threat.

The writer does communicate something quite revealing, though.

They imply that they could be someone I see every day, someone I walk by, greet, or even teach. All the smiles, the eye contact, and the social spaces of interaction — and yet there I am, just a 'nigger' to you."

The belief that black people are inferior to members of others races, especially to whites, persists for one reason. Its stubborn persistence can only be attributed to racism which is so prevalent among many whites, not just those in the United States but around the world. There is no other reason.

Professor George Yancy's ordeal is just one of the more glaring examples of the hatred that is directed against blacks by many whites across the nation everyday. Still, his case is one of the most tragic in academia where some of his white colleagues came out in their true colours to terrorise him in a diabolical scheme to intimidate him into submission but failed to achieve their goal. They could not silence him, although his traumatic experience showed how cruel his tormentors were and validated the harsh reality of what it means to be black in America.

Yet, quite often, such nefarious attempts – in a concerted effort of organised terror against blacks – accomplish exactly the opposite. And they are sometimes neutralised.

Individuals who are targeted survive the ordeal, come out stronger, and get sympathy from many people who rally to their defence, encouraging them to continue with their struggle – fighting racism or trying to achieve whatever they want to achieve even when they face virtually insurmountable obstacles. The odds may be against them but there is always a glimmer of hope they are going to succeed or, at the very least, survive.

George Yancy's identity as a black man became an unacceptable challenge to white power, and a liability to him, when he stood up and spoke the truth before a white audience of fellow scholars who were supposed to have a better understanding of the history of racism in the United States and what black people have gone through for centuries in the land of the free.

He was an embodiment of the struggle of millions of blacks facing the *same* problem and fighting the *same* war they have fought for centuries since the founding of this nation; in a country they built and whose foundation they laid from the beginning when they worked under the whip as slaves, yet where they are, even centuries later, still denied acceptance as equal citizens.

There would be no America as we know it without them. As David L. Cohn put it in *God Shakes Creation*:

"This land is first and foremost
his handiwork.
It was he who brought order
out of primeval wilderness...
Wherever one looks in this land,

whatever one sees that is the work of man,
was erected by the toiling
straining bodies of blacks." – (Reprinted in Isabel Wilkerson, *The Warmth of Other Suns: The Epic Story of America's Great Migration*, New York: Random House, 2010, p. 3).

Every adjective that has been used to describe people in a negative way, every epithet that has been thrown at them, has been used to dehumanise blacks, not just as individuals but collectively as a people, more than it has against anybody else; not against whites, not against Asians, not against any other people – except blacks in the most dehumanising way.

We are faces at the bottom of the well, as Derek Bell put it, with whites deriving satisfaction from our condition when they look down on us.

There are other people who feel the same way about us. I remember a television show on which a Hispanic woman, angry at a black man who left her, spewed racist filth, berating him: "You left me for *a black bitch on top of that?*"

She had the audacity to say all that to a black man and even hurled a double insult when she said *"on top of that?"* Leaving me is bad enough, but for *"a black bitch on top of that?"*

That is exactly what she meant, and on a national television show of all places, without mincing words.

She felt very insulted when she was replaced by a black woman. It was more than she could take – and she exploded in an outburst anger with unconstrained fury.

But it is good she did that and was honest about how she felt instead of trying to hide her prejudice and bilious rage against black people. What she said was an insult to both, black men and black women, not just to black women.

The show was a documentary and the incident was

recorded live like a news broadcast.

Her view of blacks was emblematic of the perceptions many people of other races have about us.

We are seen as worthless, the scum of the earth, good for nothing, except as objects of ridicule and contempt inflating the ego of those who think they are better than we are.

I have equally been subjected to racial indignities of all kinds, including the common insult that all blacks are "dumb," as the white deer hunter – who wasn't after deer – said to me one day.

Another white man, also talking to me, made equally stereotypical remarks about blacks in 1980. He was old enough to be my father. He said he was 52. I was 30.

One day, I was listening to soul music on a black radio station, WKWM (simply known as KWM), in Grand Rapids.

He heard the music and asked me, "What's that?" I said, "soul music." He laughed and said, "Sounds like they're trying to make a jailbreak.," and kept on laughing.

It was a typical racist remark and attitude.

The attitude was: Black people commit "all that crime," they've been locked up and they're now trying to break out jail in order to escape – so that they can go on and commit more crime as they usually do. That's how black people – "niggers" – are. What else is new?

He also invoked another racial stereotype: Black people "are loud" and made fun of soul music as well because it was "black music."

Had it been rock-and-roll, which is played mostly by whites although its origin can be traced to African American music among others, he probably would not have made fun of that.

It was also in the same year, 1980, that I had another memorable experience with racism. I was at an office of a company in Grand Rapids when an older white man who was also the supervisor asked me:

"Do you know what a computer is?"

I answered, "Yes." That's all I said to him. I think he got the message.

I had the same experience with a doctor in 1986. She was probably in her thirties, close to my age, and told me she was waiting for results on my diagnosis and was using a computer to get the results. Then she said to me, "I don't know if you know what a computer is."

I said I did. I also told her I graduated from Wayne State University. The way she looked at me, I got the impression that she didn't believe me at all when I said I graduated from college. How could she? I was black, hence ignorant, and not intelligent enough to go to college let alone graduate from an institution of higher learning.

No black person is spared such indignities, from the most humble to the most exalted including President Barack Obama.

The white doctor who had a low opinion of me as a black person who, based on her preconceived notions about blacks, probably never even heard of a computer let alone gone to college, was no exception. Others of her ilk in her profession and elsewhere have, many times, inflicted pain on untold numbers of blacks including their black colleagues.

Black doctors are equally despised by their colleagues and other nonblacks who don't believe they are intelligent enough to be doctors. It happened in Grand Rapids. It has also happened in other places across the country and continues to do so.

Even some white patients who could be in danger of losing their lives would rather wait and find a white doctor – or an Asian – than accept a black one, not only because he/she is black but also because he/she is not qualified to be a doctor.

It is a harrowing experience for black doctors and

others in the medical profession as is the case in many other fields where blacks are not considered to be good enough to do their jobs. As Teresa Weakley stated in a report, "Being Black in a White Coat: Local Doctors Face Discrimination On and Off the Job," WOOD TV 8, Grand Rapids, Michigan, 17 November 2020:

"Black Americans still make up fewer than 6% of physicians in the U.S. even though they account for 13% of the population. Those who do enter the medical field say they often encounter an unwelcoming, discriminatory environment.

In emotionally exhausting conversations with News 8, three Grand Rapids doctors who are Black shared their own experiences with racism while working and while simply living their lives. They said they were ready to speak publicly now because more people are ready to listen and they want to make a difference.

People who go through medical school put their lives on hold while their friends move forward, spending between 60 and 80 hours a week studying.

'You can't be mediocre and be a surgeon,' Dr. Charles Gibson, a board-certified trauma surgeon for Spectrum Health, explained. 'You have to be good at what you do. You have to make the grades and do the work.'

More than half of the students who apply for medical school don't get in and roughly 15% of those who do get in don't graduate. The students who get the white coat make a promise to do no harm and to do whatever they need to do to help their patients.

Still, earning that white coat doesn't always bring respect.

'The assumption is not that I'm a doctor when I walk into the room; it's just not,' Dr. Candace Smith-King, a pediatrician for Helen DeVos Children's Hospital, said.

She and Gibson, along with Dr. Kendall Hamilton, have all run into cases in which the color of their skin mattered more to their patients than their expertise, their passion or their promises.

Life on the line, patient delays surgery

In his 10 years as a trauma surgeon, Gibson has performed thousands of operations. One is burned into his memory. A woman showed up to the emergency room with a hole in her intestine.

'(It) was making her really sick. It was really painful,' Gibson said. 'She said, 'I have 12 out of 10 pain. This is the worst pain I've ever felt in my life.' So you can understand my confusion when … after going through the medical jargon and talking about the procedure, she had this kind of quizzical look on her face and said, 'Well, I understand all that, but I really don't want a Black doctor. Is there anyone else available?"

Gibson explained to the patient that there was no one else available and if she was going to have the procedure at that hospital, he would be the one to do it

'I explained to her that this isn't something you can sit on and wait until next week or even tomorrow. It's something where if we don't intervene right away, you will get worse. You will die within the next 24 hours,' Gibson said.

Still, in the worst pain she'd ever felt and knowing her life was at stake, the woman waited half an hour before she agreed to the operation.

Gibson took her to surgery and said he 'treated her just like I would treat my own mother, just like I do all of my patients.'

She survived and Gibson moved on to the next emergency, but the woman's dismissal of him because of his race stayed with him.

'It does make you think like, what am I doing differently?' he said. 'Or what could I have done better? Or did I come off wrong? All of these things that are completely irrational because racism, by definition, is irrational behavior.'"

What Dr. Gibson experienced also exposed the myth that whites in the northern part of the United States are not as racist as those in the South. Even history refutes that. There was even slavery in the North, including New York which became a bastion of liberalism together with Massachusetts and other northern states where there were also slaves and racism was just as rampant:

"Gibson experienced blatant racism like this many times growing up in the South. He and a friend noticed classmates wearing Confederate flag T-shirts to school, so they created their own T-shirts with the Confederate flag crossed out and were told that was not allowed. Police officers have called him 'boy' as an adult.

The racism isn't always so blatant.

'Even though nobody's waving a flag or burning a cross or doing anything wild, like you see on movies in the South, it doesn't mean that it's not happening,' Gibson said. 'It doesn't mean that people aren't tossing one job application and keeping another in favor of somebody that looks like them.'

He said he wants people to realize that the America they see, a land of opportunity, is a world away from what Black people may live with.

'To have the end result of all the opportunities that are presented to us, to have that sort of glass ceiling or the limits of your upward social mobility limited by something as ultimately meaningless as skin color, it's incredibly frustrating,' Gibson said.

Gibson's experiences with racism aren't limited to his time in a white coat and neither are his colleagues'.

An ally at work, treated with suspicion elsewhere

Dr. Candace Smith-King has seen the difference it can make for a patient to have a doctor who looks like them. She notices Black moms relax when she walks into the room.

'It's like, OK, I don't have to prove myself to this other Black woman who's going to help me take care of my kids. She's not going to assume that I'm trying to hurt my kids. She's going to answer my questions,' Smith-King said.

That difference goes beyond a trust or vulnerability factor. It can also change patient outcomes.

'I've had a (white) resident tell a mom to wash the child's hair every day when a Black family would never wash their child's hair every day. So when I walk in, they were like, 'So, I was told to wash his hair every day because he has this or she has this.' And I'm like, 'Yeah, you don't have to do that. Let's reframe the conversation and figure out what's feasible for the family and for you guys to do to take care of whatever's in the scalp,' Smith-King explained.

Though there have been times when she's been in a room and a patient has assumed she's a nurse, she feels respected doing her work. Things change when she leaves the hospital.

'When I take the white coat off, I really do feel as though I am not seen as a professional woman. I feel as though the assumptions that society has about Black women tend to raise themselves up,' she said.

Those assumptions often come out when she's with her children and her husband isn't there. In one case, a clerk followed her through the store as she shopped for a birthday party.

'Knowing that I was being followed around as though I

couldn't (pay), it struck a nerve with me. Actually, we just walked right out of the store,' she said. 'It's disappointing that in 2020, the assumption is that I probably can't pay for what's in my cart, and it just shouldn't be that way.'

Smith-King has four children ranging in age from 9 to 23. Her parents also live with her and she lovingly refers to them as 'two additional older children.' She pointed out that multigenerational living is common among Black families and it has led to a wonderful relationship for her children with their grandparents.

Smith-King's mom turned the tide for her family. She was the first to go to college or even finish high school, graduating in 1968 in New Orleans, a segregated city at the time.

'To see her push through, knowing that she probably did not get a wonderful education, to see her break through barriers, go to college, get her master's in social work, and then, when I was in medical school, she went back to get her Ph.D. in clinical social work. To see my mom push through like that, it made me realize there really wasn't anything that could stop me,' Smith-King said.

It's clear that family is everything to her, but with that love comes a longing for a better future for her children.

'The ache, I think, comes from having to continue to have the conversations that I know my parents have had with me and their parents have had with them,' she said. 'I feel like it's almost a ruining of their childhood experience when they realize that my skin actually matters more than who I am as a person. Having to acknowledge the fact to my 12-year-old son, who, to me, still looks like the sweetest, gentle little boy, to have to almost say, 'You're not that to anybody else, though. That's just to me and to your family, but outside this home, you are a threat.' That's the ache I feel as a mother of a Black son.'

Dr. Kendall Hamilton, a colleague of Smith-King, is an orthopedic surgeon specializing in sports medicine and arthroscopic surgery. He has spent time as the assistant team physician for several professional sports teams, including the Houston Astros and the NASA Astronaut Corps.

When he meets with a patient at his practice, it's usually someone who has a serious injury and will need further care, like surgery.

One day, he became worried because he had expected to have a consultation with a man who had been in an accident.

'After about 20 or 30 minutes had passed, the patient hadn't shown up, so I was concerned,' Hamilton recalled.

Kamie Geerling is the operations manager for the office. An athletic trainer came to her about the patient who was supposed to see Hamilton. The patient wanted another doctor.

'I honestly didn't know what to do,' she said. 'I've never experienced it. I was just shocked that someone would say, 'I don't want to see that provider because he's Black.' I was absolutely shaken. I went back to my office and cried. I was just frustrated and confused.'

She didn't tell Hamilton because she was trying to protect him.

'I went in and talked to the patient and let him know that he could not choose his doctor based on discriminatory reasons,' Geerling said.

When Hamilton asked the staff to reach out to the patient because he had not shown for his appointment, they told him that he did show up but they took care of the situation. The doctor didn't accept that and they eventually told him the truth.

'They wanted to protect me from hearing that story,' Hamilton said. 'We immediately got our risk and legal team and some of our senior leadership team involved just to get some clarification about, legally, how could we still support this patient or help this patient but at the same time not honor any requests that were based on discrimination.'

Hamilton said he was impressed with the support he got from Spectrum Health leaders, who told him that he was correct in his assessment that racism wasn't a legal reason to not see a physician.

But it doesn't change what happened.

'It's hard. It hurts, because I can get more training, I can get more education, I can get better at what I do with experience and practice, but I can't change how I look. I can't change my skin color. I can't change how I was born,' he said. 'So it does hurt. It's always with you. It sticks with you.'

A new push for racial equity

The death of George Floyd at the hands of a Minneapolis police officer earlier this year sparked protests across the country calling for police reform.

In Grand Rapids, Smith-King struggled.

'Watching him die and going to work and not hearing anybody at work talk about it, not seeing any emails go out like, what just happened in our country?' she said. 'Having to go to work and just function was probably one of the lowest points in my life. By that Friday, I sent an email out to everybody I knew who I could email at Spectrum and I said, 'The silence is deafening.''

Spectrum Health President and CEO Tina Freese Decker called Smith-King within an hour of her sending the email and asked what the hospital could do to support its team members and what they should do to work on changing the health care system. Freese Decker had already drafted an email to send to the staff that day.

'It made me feel better knowing that I wasn't on an island by myself, because that's how it felt at the time,' Smith-King said....

Spectrum had already initiated plans to improve diversity and equity, joining the #123forEquity Campaign and establishing a diversity officer position in 2018.

Ovell Barbee, who grew up in Grand Rapids and returned after spending 15 years in other parts of the country, currently holds that role and is also the senior vice president of human resources for Spectrum.

'I recognize that, as a leader, oftentimes I'm sitting in rooms, and I may be the only person who looks like me in that forum,' Barbee said. 'I feel a duty and an obligation to represent individuals who look like me, who may not be sitting at the table.'

On Nov. 9, he was named to the National Diversity Council's Board of Directors for the National Coalition for Racial Justice and Equity because of his work in Grand Rapids, which included a call to 'Stop the Silence.' He spent a year meeting with leaders in the area to understand the perceptions and attitudes toward Spectrum Health. The most measurable commitment the system has made is promising at least $100 million over the next 10 years to accelerate and expand efforts in addressing racial and ethnic health inequities."

Racism experienced by doctors and other medical professionals in Grand Rapids is only a part of a larger problem problem of systemic racism in a country whose very foundation was racism and racial inequality.

It is a problem that manifests itself in the most glaring and vicious ways when black people encounter white police officers and others including Asian and Hispanic who are are just as racist towards blacks.

The brutal murder of George Floyd by a white police officer in Minneapolis, Minnesota, recorded and televised worldwide, jolted the conscience of tens of millions of people as never before. The country had never witnessed such a groundswell of support for racial justice since the civil rights movement in the sixties. As Teresa Weakley further stated in her report on racism against black doctors in Grand Rapids:

"Floyd's death was only the most recent incident in a long history of police brutality in the U.S., but his story garnered more national attention than many others. Smith-King attributes that to the (coronavirus) pandemic.

'The pace is slow… without COVID, George Floyd could have just been like Trayvon Martin, the Sandra Blands and the other Black people who have been killed needlessly, you know?' she said. 'I definitely think the slowness of the pace because of the pandemic allowed our experiences to be heard.'

She was involved in the uncomfortable conversations Spectrum Health hosted to better understand what employees were dealing with, as was Gibson.

'We've had tough conversations where they've asked people like me and others, Black nurses or social workers or surgeons, to say like, 'What's going on? Do we have a blind spot here? Is there something we're missing in our own house?" Gibson said.

Sometimes, yes, Gibson said.

He recalled a situation in which he spoke with a co-worker who was dealing with a family going through the difficult process of making a decision about organ donation.

'(He) said to me, 'I could just put on some black paint and then talk to the family and see if that would make them feel better.' And he thought it was a joke and kind of chuckled. I was just dumbfounded. I didn't say anything. I didn't even know how to react,' Gibson said.

That person is no longer employed at Spectrum Health, but Gibson referenced it as one of the things Black people worry about when they go for care.

'It's become more and more zero tolerance for this sort of thing. There are two sides to a story every time, but if we vet the story and figure out that it truly did happen the way people are saying, then there's just no place for that anywhere, but certainly not at Spectrum Health,' he said.

The conversations with co-workers have included questions about what they can do to improve equity in their lives.

Smith-King has suggested looking at what books they read in their families, where their children play on the playground, who they surround themselves with and decide if everyone looks like them or there is a good mix of people, socially and economically. She encourages everyone to be involved in their children's education and find out who is on the school board, making decisions about what they learn in class.

Gibson suggested not bringing up big topics with new friends right away but rather inviting them to lunch and building a relationship so that when more serious topics come up it's easier to have a genuine conversation.

'People do care, they just don't always know how to approach the problem,' Gibson said. 'I've told my other (Black) colleagues that you can't sound the alarm and say we want this change, and then when we get people who are willing to step outside of their comfort zones, we have to be sensitive to the fact that they may need a little help, a little guidance.'

Inequity as a health crisis

All three doctors see glimmers of hope in the quest for change, but get frustrated with the pace.

Smith-King pointed to how quickly the hospital shifted to respond to COVID-19.

'It was overnight. They set up a command center and we had 10 teams doing 10 different things,' she said. 'The same thing should happen with systemic racism in health care.

'I have to realize that it's going to take time to change culture, but the fact that not only has the seed been planted, it's watered and I tend to see it coming out of the ground, it's going to take a while for it to grow, but it's coming,' she continued.

'I think the awareness is there,' Hamilton said of progress. 'We're still having the conversation about what activism looks like, but I think awareness is one of the first major key steps.'

Gibson's final statement on the matter was a powerful one, a call to stand not behind those fighting for change but instead side by side and make it a movement and not a moment:

'Understand that we've been screaming at the top of our lungs about injustice and racism and oppression and things like that for over 450 years,' he said. 'Welcome to the party."'

One of the most painful realities of being black is the refusal by many whites – as well as many other nonblacks – to accept black people as equal human beings endowed with intelligence just like other human beings and equally entitled to dignity and respect.

There is a persistent rejection of black people, a rejection with an emphasis on: Everybody is welcome, "except blacks." Everybody is accepted – "except niggers." Everybody is fine – "except niggers." We can work with everybody else – "except blacks." "No niggers allowed," reminiscent of the admonition in sundown towns to "niggers" to get out of town before the sun goes down.

Many blacks are painfully aware of that: "They accept everybody else except us." "They are really cruel." "After all what we have been through?"

It goes on and on.

As black people, we don't even have simple common sense, according to this logic.

I have been through all that in my life as a black man. I cite a few incidents to illustrate that.

It was because I was black that one white man did not think I even had simple common sense to do what I was getting ready to do. He felt he had to come to my rescue, uninvited, to show me how to do it.

I was at the main post office in Grand Rapids in 1988 when I had an encounter with a white man who was probably in his late seventies or eighties.

I was getting ready to use a copy machine to make some copies when he approached me. He had been standing only a few feet away from where I was and was starting to walk away when he saw me at the copy machine. He turned around and came towards me after he saw I had some papers in my hand and concluded – and rightly so – I was getting ready to make some copies.

I was looking at the copier getting ready to put some coins in the slot when he came over and told me, pointing at the slot, "You put it in there," assuming I didn't know where to put in the money. I had not asked for any help from anybody. He didn't even wait to see what I was going to do and automatically assumed I didn't know how to use a copy machine simply because I was black.

I did not say anything to him and simply put some coins in the slot, pressed the button (it was too late for him to instruct me on how to do that), and made the copies I wanted to make and walked away.

He sounded as if he had a foreign accent, not American. But he could have been American-born and brought up in the United States. Americans from different parts of the country have different accents – his wasn't Southern which is very distinct and easily recognisable.

He could have had an American accent I was not familiar with – from Appalachia, the Ozarks or some other part of the United States. He clearly did not have a Midwestern accent. I would have known; that's the accent of Midwesterners including those where born or brought up in Michigan which is one of the states in a region known as the Midwest.

Whatever the case, it would have made no difference, none at all, even if he came from another country. He was white. I was black. That was the difference. Many whites from other countries are just as racist towards blacks.

It is slights like that which cumulatively have an impact on black people which is as effective as using crude language calling them "niggers."

Some of them don't even answer blacks when they greet them.

Contempt for blacks, including total disregard of their dignity as equal human beings, takes many forms, including simply ignoring their presence even during verbal exchanges.

It may be at a multiracial gathering in an informal setting where the presence of blacks is no more than a salve for the conscience of some whites who feel guilty of mistreating black people for centuries.

They have planned the event, and have invited blacks, for no other reason than that; roughly equivalent to how many whites felt when they voted for Barack Obama to become the first black president in American history.

Many of them voted for him for different reasons. But there were also those who voted for him to atone for their sins against black people – historical and contemporary.

Some of them have supposedly experienced a spiritual rebirth after mistreating blacks for so long. Yet, the transformation some of them have undergone is more apparent than real.

Even verbal exchanges between individuals can be humiliating. Some whites talk to black people, full-grown blacks, as if they are talking to children. They even treat and regard them as if they are children because they have no respect for them; the level of their intelligence – of full-grown black men and women – being equated to that of white children. Or they simply ignore them as if they don't even exist.

I have had that kind of experience. I remember when I was a student at Wayne State University in the early seventies, I was at a gathering of some whites – taken there by a member of my host family in Bay City, who was the husband and father – where another foreign student from China or one of the other Oriental countries, was also invited. He was also a guest of one of the families in the area as part of an international exchange programme.

During conversations, I was almost completely ignored by them. All the whites who were there, about six to eight of them, were old enough to be our parents. They hardly looked at me. Their focus was on the Oriental student. The conversations were also among themselves but they showed great interest in the Oriental student, asking him questions about his education, what he was studying, where he came from, and so on.

I remember very well only one lady asked me: "What are you studying?" That was the end of it except for occasional chats with the member of my host family who took me there. He was also the one who introduced me to them. Yet no one asked me about my country or about Africa. And I knew why. As a black man, my presence meant absolutely nothing to them. And I was nothing to them.

My dignity was not wounded. I was dignified enough not to be offended by people who did not want to talk to me. And they didn't have to.

That is why any black person who respects himself should not want to integrate with people who don't want to integrate with him.

Their moral bankruptcy is their badge of honour. No dignified black man, or anybody person of conscience, should want to wear it together with them.

I have been subjected to other racial indignities through the years, some of which are similar to what happened to me in Bay City 46 years ago in 1974.

In the late 1990s, a white man who was a friend of the son of an African American woman I knew deliberately ignored me when I called his name. I wanted to ask him just one simple question about something. He simply ignored me and looked the other way when he heard me call his name. He ignored me as if I did not even exist. Yet there I was, almost right in front of him, only a few feet away from where he was sitting. He was in their house. Yet he did not have the decency to behave in a civil manner or acknowledge my presence. He had crude manners and was very rude.

After he left, I told them what happened. They were equally offended. Fortunately, he never went back to visit them and I never saw him again.

In the early 2000s, a white wife of a Hispanic man I knew ignored me when I greeted her in the presence of her husband. She just stared at me, without uttering a word, and simply ignored my greeting. Her facial expression also showed she was angry with me just for greeting her.

It was during the same period when another white man, who was in the house of my African American friend, also ignored me when I greeted him. It was only the two of us during that moment. He just glanced at me and did not acknowledge my greeting. He heard me. He had no hearing problem. I knew him. My African American friend was also offended by his behaviour.

A racial insult to one black person is an insult to all blacks. Race is indivisible; so is humanity.

Cumulatively, such insults demonstrate the scope and persistence of racism. It is a major problem between individuals as much as it is at the institutional level. And it has compromised the nation's ideals and character.

When you multiply the number of these incidents of

racism with the number of black people who experience basically the same thing, you realise racism still is a major problem in every city and every state across the nation. It happens everyday to millions of blacks, one incident or another in which a black person is insulted or humiliated. And the total number of white racists is not negligible; it's probably millions of them in a country with a population of more than 300 million, the vast majority of whom are white.

As a black person, sometimes you are victimised without even knowing that you have been a victim of racism. You may find out later you couldn't get somethings done, not because they just couldn't be done then even by a white person; or you were denied employment or housing not because no vacancy was available; or you face other problems not because other people including whites also face the same problems; you went through all that – couldn't get things done, couldn't get a job or a house to rent or buy – because you were black and for no other reason.

All blacks have faced this problem, sometimes even unknowingly helping their victimisers to victimise them and even end up defending them: "The apartment just wasn't ready to be rented." "The company is not hiring anymore – there are even some blacks who work there, I saw them, therefore it had nothing to with racism when I wasn't hired" – only to find out later some whites were hired soon after you left.

There is not a single black person who has not been a victim of racism. It pervades society.

It is an integral part of life, of the black experience in the American context, and may sometimes be overlooked and even ignored by the victims because they know that is just the way things are, just the way life is, yet without condoning such injustices.

Africans who come to the United States, I being one of them, suffer the same racial injustices although some of them delude themselves into believing that whites like them better than they do American blacks; an attitude, and sheer naiveté, which has led to strains in relations between some of them. It's not many of them who think that way but they do exist.

Racist whites don't care about them anymore than they do their brethren, African Americans. You came from Africa, so what? – you're just another nigger to them. They don't even want you here anymore than they do American-born blacks and wish you had never come here and should have stayed over there, in the "jungle," rubbing shoulders with animals.

I remember one white man, an authority figure on campus and old enough to be my father, who was extremely rude to me in Detroit in 1974 when he learned I had been awarded a merit scholarship because I did well in school at Wayne State University. It was partial scholarship and just for one term. He was angry because I had been given such assistance and said to me: "You did not come here in chains like your ancestors!"

It was clear he meant I should not have come here and should have stayed in Africa. He also implied had I been born born and brought up in the Untied States, I may have have been entitled to some kind of financial assistance for my education – to pay tuition, buy some books and so forth.

These are some of the whites some Africans who come to the United States think they care about them and like them better or more than they do American blacks. No, they don't.

Many whites including liberals – friends of Negroes – don't even want to pay African Americans reparations; they don't even think about making *any* amends, in *any* form, for slavery, let alone help Africans who come here.

Racism is pervasive and it favours none of its victims including blacks from other countries who live in the United States. It doesn't even spare its perpetrators who are victims of their own sins and depravity as purveyors of evil against black people as if they have no conscience man is endowed with. That is the nature of racism. It dehumanises both its victims and perpetrators.

And it includes the belief, prevalent among many whites, that black people don't even have simple common sense to do simple things such as using a copy machine on their own unless they are instructed how to do it, as the white man at the main Grand Rapids post office implied I couldn't. Many of them also believe we can't even count, do well in school or, in the case of African Americans, even learn English although it is their native language as Americans born and brought up in the United States.

The list goes on and on; it is a litany of insults, repeated by racists and even by some enlightened liberals because of their paternalistic attitude towards blacks.

It all has to do with the intellectual capacity of black people. The assumption, and belief, is that we are mental weaklings, hence mentally deficient, because we are genetically inferior to whites and to members of other races. We are on the lowest rung of the evolutionary ladder.

It is raw-naked racism harboured even by some of the most "enlightened" members of society. Some of them even express it, freely, in their encounters with black people. And they don't even care what some of the blacks they talk to have accomplished in life.

There are many whites and other nonblacks who would not believe me if I told them I have written some books which are used in colleges and universities around the world. They are in their libraries. They are also found in public libraries.

I don't claim or pretend to be a great writer or scholar. It is just a fact that my books are used in institutions of higher learning and by members of the general public round the globe. Yes, I am black. Yes, I write in English. Yes, I learned English in Africa and was first taught by black African teachers. Yes, I was born and brought up in Africa. And yes, I came to the United States to go to college.

The two whites who asked me if I knew what a computer was, the one who said he watched a movie "full of coloured folks – all of them *dumb*," and the one at the post office who thought I did not know how to use a copy machine, would be some of the people who would not believe that I have written some books.

They probably would *never* believe me even if I told them I wrote some books, or wrote *anything* – in my national language Kiswahili (Swahili) which I also taught in Detroit and in Grand Rapids in the early and mid-seventies.

Those are just a few examples of my encounters with raw-naked racism; I have had others that were subtle.

And that was not the end of my encounters with overt racism.

I have had other memorable experiences with racism in the United States.

In the summer of 1983 when an African immigrant and I were on our way from Grand Rapids to Greensboro, North Carolina, coincidentally, the first American city I went to when I first came to the United States in 1972, we stopped to get some rest somewhere in Virginia. It was in the evening, before sunset, and had the car parked beside the road.

As we stood out there, we saw a car going in the opposite direction. Whites were in the car. They seemed to be young – in their teens or twenties, may be even in their thirties – but they could have been older.

When they saw us, we couldn't tell how many were in the car, they slowed down and yelled at us and kept on saying something, yelling, in an angry tone. We couldn't tell exactly what they said but it sounded like a drawn-out racial slur "niggers," shouted at us by different occupants of the car.

Whatever they said, it was probably highly offensive directed against us because we were black. There seemed to be no other reason. Why did they yell at us? And so loudly?

In 1980, a fellow African and I went to look for an apartment in a predominantly white suburb of Kentwood which is an integral part of the Grand Rapids metropolitan area. Before going there, my colleague called the manager of the apartment building; in fact, he called from my telephone in my apartment in the inner city of Grand Rapids, the ghetto, and he was the one who was looking for a place to rent.

The manager, a female, told him the apartment was available and he could go and see it. But when we went there, as soon as she saw us, she said, "The apartment has been rented." That was just within half an hour or so after we called and were assured the apartment was available for rent. Obviously it was but not to blacks.

Sometime later, in the same year, we went to look for an apartment in a building that was very close to a predominantly black area in Grand Rapids; it was on the borderline of the inner city in an area known as Heritage Hill which is a historic district with some old mansions and expensive houses owned or rented mostly by whites in a predominantly white city which was once very conservative and a Republican stronghold.

I went in and knocked on the door of the building manager's apartment. A white lady, old enough to be my mother, opened the door. As soon as she saw me, she asked, "Paper boy?" Reminiscent of the racial insult many whites routinely used in the past, and even today although less frequently, calling full-grown black men, "boys" – "hey, boy," "shut up, boy," "sit down, boy," "pick that up, boy,""be careful, boy," "what's your name, boy?," "did you hear me, boy?" and so on. In fact, I have had that experience of being called a "boy."

In 1988, a non-white Hispanic man – he was Puerto

Rican – and I were driving from Detroit to Grand Rapids. We stopped at a rest area on the highway to use the restroom. When we were inside, four white men walked in, also to use the restroom. One of them who was about my age or younger said to us, "Hey, be careful where you park your car, boys." He called us "boys" two more times, once saying "you boys."

The Hispanic man I was with was the one who was driving. And he did nothing wrong. He parked his car at the rest area the way any car was supposed to be parked.

The white was being extremely provocative as if he wanted to start a fight. The other whites who were with him were just smiling and kept on smiling. They obviously shared his sentiments.

There we were, two full-grown men, being called "boys" by a white man who obviously had no respect for black people and other nonwhites – none whatsoever. He saw us as beneath him just because he was white and we were not.

I was 38 years old. The Hispanic man was about 60, old enough to be my father and the white man's father; still, that made no difference to him.

That white man would never have called us "boys" had we been white – the Hispanic driver didn't even do anything wrong when he parked his car at the rest area; even if he did, it would have been unthinkable for the white man to call him – a 60-year-old man or someone old enough to be his father – a "boy" had he been white.

Black women are not spared this kind of humiliation black men are subjected to and which they have to endure at the hands of some whites who call them "boys." I knew one such victim in Grand Rapids.

She went to see a white doctor who condescendingly called her "girl." That was in 1988, the same year in which I was insulted and called a "boy."

She was 42 years old. She had an appointment with the doctor and when she went to see him, he said to her, loudly, "Sit down, girl!" "Sit down!" He yelled at her for nothing.

She found the doctor on her own and her mother, who was driving, took her to see him. Her mother was waiting in another room and also heard the doctor humiliate her daughter.

Just seeing a black person in his office infuriated him. It triggered something in him and had bilious rage flowing out of him, vented at the black woman.

She had a lawsuit during that time and wanted some medical records to validate her claim for monetary compensation and having her medical bills paid.

Unfortunately, the doctor she found was not the right one because she was not the right patient for him simply because she was not white.

The medical report he wrote about her condition did not even help her with her lawsuit. It was a bad report.

She still won her case, eventually, using medical reports from other doctors who supported her claim that her medical condition was very bad because of what happened to her.

She suffered permanent physical impairment.

The racist doctor who yelled at her – "sit down, girl!" – didn't see it that way.

He said there was nothing wrong with her; other doctors said there was; he also said she could go back to work; other doctors said she couldn't.

More than 30 years later, she was still in the same condition: physically impaired. He condition also got worse through the years.

When she told her lawyer who was representing her in the lawsuit about what happened when he went to see the doctor, he said he knew the doctor. He was a white lawyer and said he had a number of black clients who had seen the same doctor before.

He said whenever a black person went to see that doctor, there were always complaints about him because of the way he mistreated black patients. He had no respect for black people and was known for his racist behaviour and making derogatory remarks that were clearly racist.

This provides the context in which the white apartment manager called me "paper boy" in 1980.

Black people are still not accorded respect by many whites as equal human beings.

The apartment building manager probably already knew the person – the boy – who delivered the newspaper, *The Grand Rapids Press*, to the building everyday.

I was 30 years old when she called me "boy." But even if she mistook me for a teenager, which I don't believe she did, considering my maturity and how I communicated with her as a full-grown man, it was her response to my enquiry about an apartment that said it all.

I asked her, "Do you have an apartment for rent?" She responded: "Only when someone dies." Which wasn't true. People had been moving in and out of the building through the years, alive, and there were times when apartments were available for rent in there.

The Fair Housing Act prohibiting discrimination in housing and which was passed in 1968 following the riots which rocked the nation when Dr. Martin Luther King was assassinated, meant absolutely nothing to the white manager and others who had managed the apartment building before her. And it meant nothing to other landlords as well across the nation; it still doesn't to many of them.

That was not the end of my experience with racial discrimination. I faced more in the following years. But when I looked for a place to rent in the ghetto, I had no problem finding one because that is where black people were supposed to live in a segregated area.

When I was in the ghetto during that time, I lived in a house owned by a black lady who was old enough to be my mother. I lived upstairs and she lived downstairs. I had no problems with her. but racial problems were waiting for me elsewhere.

In 1989, an African American and I were twice denied places to rent because we were black.

One was in Grandville, a suburb of Grand Rapids and overwhelmingly white, where we wanted to rent a house.

We talked to the owner on the telephone and he told us we could go and see the house. He said he would be there to show it to us. And he was, when we arrived. But he told us the house was not available for rent right then. That was not what he told us earlier. Once he saw us, black, that was the end of it.

Some whites who knew him confirmed to us that the landlord, a white, was a racist and did not want to rent to any blacks.

One white man, who was also a landlord, told the African American a few years before than that white landlords really didn't want to rent to blacks. But they sometimes rented to them because they were forced to do so under the law. He said he knew many of them and heard what they said. That is also what he heard many times when he was with fellow whites including landlords.

Our experience in Grandville was not an isolated incident. It was the same experience we had in Eastown, an enclave in Grand Rapids, which had a reputation of being very liberal in a conservative city and still does.

It is also known as the Greenwich Village of Grand Rapids and is very close to an affluent area, East Grand Rapids, which is also overwhelmingly white. East Grand Rapids was also the home of former United States President Gerald Ford and is a part of the Grand Rapids metropolitan area.

Eastown was also very close to a predominantly black area where I lived between 1976 and 1977.

There was an advertisement in the newspaper, *The Grand Rapids Press*, stating the apartment we wanted to look at in Eastown was available for rent. That was in 1989.

We went there and were shown the apartment. But the person who showed it to us, a young white man close to my age, gave all kinds of excuses – in terms of additional expenses, including higher rent, maintenance costs and so on – to make sure we would be discouraged from saying to him, "Yes, we will take it." We did not and left.

I was in the same area of Eastown where one day in 1979 I witnessed a racial incident in which one of my former roommates, an African American, was involved; we were roommates from the summer of 1976 until 1977.

We went to a bar, the Intersection, one evening, to have some beer; it was during summer.

The bar was near the intersection of Lake Drive SE (Southeast) and Wealthy Street SE right on the edge of the affluent suburb of East Grand Rapids which is considered to be a separate city although it is within the Grand Rapids metropolitan area.

We were sitting at the counter and drinking some beer when a young white man walked in. There were other whites at the counter but no other blacks except us.

The young white man – he seemed to be about my age, in the late twenties – who had just walked in stood next to my friend, with his hands on the counter, and ordered some beer. It was around 5 PM and he seemed to have just come from work. He was dressed like someone who worked in an office and wore a necktie.

My friend tried to start a conversation with him and the young white man looked at him straight face and told him: "I don't like blacks."

My friend, aware of the racial stereotypes about blacks being branded as "bad people" in every conceivable way tried – in a disgusting way, as I saw it – to impress the young white man by telling him, "All of us are not the same."

I thought that was really, really disgusting, literally begging the young white man to accept us as black people.

The young white man was not impressed and rebuffed

him. He gave him a curt response: "It makes no difference to me. I still don't like blacks. I don't."

We did not stay long at the bar and left after we finished drinking our beer.

I was very familiar with the bar from the time when I was a student at Aquinas College three years earlier in 1976. It was a watering hole for Aquinas College students, black and white. We used to go there now and then to drink some beer.

It was also in the same year when I was a student at Aquinas College, in the summer of 1976, when another racial incident took place at the same bar.

I went to the bar one afternoon with a young white man – we were about the same age – who worked at Aquinas College. He was not a student. We worked together on campus just as I did with a few of my fellow students.

When we walked into the bar, there was an older white man, old enough to be our father, sitting alone at a table and drinking some beer. The young white man I was with knew him and went straight to the table for us to join him. We sat down and ordered some beer.

When he heard I came from Africa, he started talking about white people in South Africa and how they had developed the country, implying "unlike blacks." He went further and said they treated blacks well and there was nothing wrong with apartheid – it was good for all South Africans. He was very defensive of apartheid. I took the opposite view.

Not long after that, there was a conference on apartheid South Africa held at Aquinas College; and there he was, attending the meeting. I remember he stood up and spoke briefly again defending apartheid. He drew murmurs from the audience, almost all-white.

The main speaker was a Catholic priest who was also a professor at Aquinas College. He vehemently condemned apartheid and even spoke very highly of other African countries which were helping black people and other nonwhites in South Africa to fight apartheid. He went on to say Africa was one like the Untied States and white South Africans had no right trying to separate their country – even if not physically – from the rest of the continent.

Also on the opposite side, besides the older white man whom I first met at the bar in Eastown and who also briefly spoke at the conference defending apartheid, was a white student attending Aquinas College. He also strongly defended apartheid and drew furious responses from some members of the audience. He even cited Aristotle and the Bible in defence of his arguments to justify slavery and apartheid. He was very clear about his position: black people were not equal to whites, should not live with whites, and were meant to be servants and slaves of white people.

The rest of the participants, including Catholic nuns who also taught at Aquinas College – one of them was my professor in a philosophy class – vehemently condemned apartheid.

The conference was even covered by one local television station, WZZM 13. I also ended up on television.

I saw the cameraman focusing on where I was sitting, with whites, and didn't know I was going to be on television until later that evening when I was watching the news.

One of my students at South Middle School where I taught Swahili also watched the news and was excited about it. She said she saw me on television and was glad to see one of her teachers on there. I told her it was good she watched the news and saw what happened at Aquinas on that day because it was a very important conference on racism in South Africa.

I was just one of the people who attended the conference and did not make any significant contribution to the discussion. I just happened to be one of the few blacks who attended the meeting at a predominantly white school. And that explains why the television camera man focused on where I was sitting "in a sea" of whites who were there to take part in a conference on the plight of black people and other nonwhites in apartheid South Africa.

What was important to me about the news broadcast on the conference at Aquinas College was the involvement of Americans of *all* races in the campaign against the racist policies of the South African regime, giving me encouragement that there was widespread condemnation of the abominable and abhorrent institution of apartheid and its diabolical policies and there would be a day when the walls of the citadel of white supremacy on the African continent would come tumbling down. And they did.

That was one of my most memorable experiences of my student days at Aquinas College. And it fuelled my optimism, especially as an African, that apartheid would end one day, as it indeed did, less than twenty years later in 1994.

But there is still racism in South Africa almost 30 years after apartheid ended just as there is racism in the United States more than 50 years after the civil rights movement. Grand Rapids is no exception in spite of the fact that the city has become somewhat liberal through the years – more liberal than it was when I first came here from Detroit in 1976, although some people, especially blacks in the inner city, dispute that. They say Grand Rapids *still* is a conservative city. People sharply differ on that.

Even at the conference on apartheid at Aquinas, there may have been some participants who were sympathetic to the apartheid regime for racial reasons besides the two who were vocal in their support of white domination of nonwhites in South Africa. But the prevailing sentiment at the conference was that apartheid was wrong.

It was a sentiment that was echoed across the nation.

Even Aquinas College students who mingled at the bar in Eastown – coincidentally, in an area known as a liberal oasis – expressed liberal views in general. I also lived in the Eastown area twice, at different times in 1976 and 1977, for a combined period of about one year and a half. The part where I lived was almost all-black.

A few years after I left Aquinas College, I was at the same bar in Eastown, still popular with Aquinas College students, when another racial incident took place, although outside the bar. It was in the summer of 1981.

An African American friend of mine and I went to the bar one afternoon. When we came out of the bar and were getting ready to go into his car, a white man across the street saw us and shouted: "Hey, you niggers got some weed?"

He was getting ready to go into a bar across the street from the one we had just left. He seemed to be in his late twenties or early thirties, not much older or younger than we were.

We did not say anything to him. We just ignored him and went into the car and left.

Apart from using a highly offensive racial insult against us, that white man – who seemed to be our age, may be only a few years apart – demonstrated the utter callousness many whites have towards blacks even on highly sensitive matters which have to do with race.

He also reinforced a racial stereotype about black people as drug users. Simply because we were black, he automatically assumed we smoked and sold marijuana, as many whites believe blacks, especially young black men, do.

If you are black and you tell them you don't smoke weed, the response you get from them is, "We know how you guys are."

That's exactly what someone I knew in Grand Rapids was told by one of his white co-workers. He was born and brought up in Africa and had a white-collar job at one of the major companies in this city on the banks of the Grand River.

One day, one of his white co-workers who shared an office with him asked him for some "weed," while pretending to be smoking a marijuana cigarette and playing with his left ear, pointing behind the ear – between the ear cup and the skull – where some weed smokers keep their "joints" (weed cigarettes), usually just one at a time.

The black employee said he didn't smoke weed. His white co-worker didn't believe him and, while smiling, told the black man: "Come on, we know you guys."

That is the attitude of many whites towards blacks. If you are black, especially, a young black man, it is hard for them to believe you don't smoke weed or use some other kind of drug or drugs.

The racial insult – "Hey, you niggers got some weed?" – that was hurled at me and my African American friend also did not surprise me. I knew there were many whites who felt that way about blacks.

I had another unpleasant experience with racism when I moved from the southeast side to the northeast side of Grand Rapids; more were yet to come.

I moved there from the Heritage Hill Historic District which is described as one of the largest urban historic districts in the country with homes dating from 1848 and designed in more than 60 architectural styles. I lived in the Heritage Hill area for a little more than two years from July 1990 to August 1992.

My encounter with racism took place at another residence very close to the one where I first lived when I moved to the northeast side.

In January 1993, an African American and I found an apartment in an integrated middle-class neighbourhood in that part of Grand Rapids. The neighbourhood is in Midtown, near downtown. The area is also a commercial district. The place where we lived was about one mile from downtown.

Although integrated, the northeast side was still predominantly white, as the city itself was and still is. I lived in that area for many years.

Even after many years, the area was still mostly white; the ghetto, the inner city, still predominantly black and poor, a product of structural racism.

Two days after we moved into the apartment, three white men came to our door in broad daylight. Two of them kicked the door hard and yelled, "We don't want no niggers here." Then they ran away.

They didn't care it was daytime and other tenants saw and heard them. They did not even live in the same apartment building we did. They lived in another building right next door but on the same premises. Both were owned by the same landlord.

Another racial incident took place on the same premises two years later.

A young black couple, African American, rented an apartment in the same building in which we lived. They did not stay long and when they moved out, the landlord complained about them and said the apartment was dirty. He said that to some white tenants, men and women, and one racially mixed woman who was also one of the tenants, when they were standing in front of the building one afternoon.

The racially mixed woman, in response to the landlord, said: "That is how black people are." And they all laughed when she said that. The landlord also laughed.

The laughter said it all. It was a sweeping indictment against all blacks as "dirty" people.

It was also an endorsement of a racial stereotype about blacks so common among many whites and even among other people who are not black, such as the woman I just mentioned who seemed to be of white, Hispanic and Native American ancestry. The stereotype is: "Black people are not clean. They are dirty. They are irresponsible. And that's just the way they are."

Not long after that, we wanted to move and tried to rent an apartment in the same area.

The apartment was very close to where we lived and it would have been very easy for us to move to our new residence.

We called the owner of the apartment and told him one of us would be there in a few minutes to look at it. It was within walking distance, only about three minutes.

He told us he was already there and would show it to us. He said he lived in the same building and was waiting to show the apartment to prospective tenants.

A very close relative of my African American friend who was staying with us during that time went to look at the apartment on our behalf.

When he got there, he looked through the window upstairs and saw someone. It was the landlord since he said he was already there to show the apartment to prospective tenants. The landlord also saw him.

When my friend's relative knocked on the door, he got no response; he knocked again, and again, and still got no response.

The landlord saw it was a black man at the door who said he wanted to look at the apartment and that was the end of it. He did not even go downstairs to talk to him. He stayed upstairs and my friend's relative saw him up there when he was leaving.

My friend's relative started walking back to where we lived and stopped for a moment. When he looked back, he saw some whites going to the same apartment house he had just left. He even heard them knocking on the door. The landlord opened the door for them right away.

There was no doubt in his mind, and in ours, that they were prospective tenants and the landlord let them in because he wanted to rent the apartment only to whites.

That was in the mid-1990s, long after the civil rights movement had transformed America into a better society in terms of rights for black people.

Yet, laws against racial discrimination in housing and public facilities meant absolutely nothing to the landlord even decades after they were passed.

That is what an African American woman I knew well experienced in Grand Rapids in the sixties; American blacks were then simply known as "black Americans" or "Afro-Americans."

One day in the late sixties,, the African American woman went to look at an apartment in the Eastown area. She went with her aunt, her mother's younger sister, and her aunt's husband who looked white; he was partly black, about one-eighth, but looked white because he was mostly white. He was the one who was driving.

When they got there, the African American woman went to the apartment house and knocked on the door. When the white landlord saw her, he told her the apartment had just been rented. She did not believe him. She went back to the car and told her aunt and her uncle what happened. They also did not believe the landlord. They knew why she had been told the apartment had just been rented.

Her uncle drove away with them in the car and parked it just a few yards away around the corner where the white landlord could not see it. He then went back to the apartment house. When he knocked on the door, the white landlord opened the door. He asked the landlord if the apartment was still available for rent. The landlord said, "Yes."

The black woman later found a house in the inner city where her neighbour next door was a white lady who was old enough to be her grandmother. She was a racist but liked talking to her new black neighbour although she did not like black people.

The black woman said she also liked talking to her because, as a strong Christian, she had compassion for her and saw her as a grandmother who deserved respect because of her advanced age.

When the black woman's aunt and her husband went to visit her one day, her white neighbour asked her who that white man was. She told her that was her uncle who was married to her aunt, her mother's younger sister. She also told her he was not just white – he was also black.

She didn't believer her. She just stared at her in disbelief. She did not believe has was also black or partly black. She thought it was just a white man who was with a black woman and didn't like that – let alone the fact that he was married to her.

The white woman also told her new black neighbour that she knew a nine-year-old black boy who liked talking to her whenever he went by her house, crying on her shoulder. She said the boy would cry on her shoulder and tell her, "Why are my people so bad!"

It was not a question but an admission of a painful reality about the "nature" of black people by a nine-year-old!

The old white lady told that story a number of times and even mentioned the name of a black church, one of the largest in Grand Rapids, she claimed the boy and her family belonged to. She also named the pastor of the church to make her story even more convincing.

Neither was true – about a black boy crying on her shoulder and about the boy being a member of the black church she mentioned and whose pastor she also named.

The black woman didn't believe her. And when she told her uncle – and her aunt – what the old white lady said, that she knew a black boy who often cried on her shoulder telling her why his people were so bad, her uncle said "that woman has been prejudiced all her life. No black boy went to her crying on her shoulder and told her 'why are my people so bad!'" He also said nine-year-olds and other children don't even talk like that.

She made up the whole thing. It was a downright lie. There was no black boy who went to her, crying on her shoulder and telling her, 'why are my people so bad!" The boy did not exist.

But she expressed a collective sentiment shared by

millions of whites about black people being criminals and good for nothing.

She also complained about blacks moving into the city and forcing whites to move out. Her black neighbour told her they didn't have to leave.

It was a part of the phenomenon of white flight which accelerated and reached its peak in the seventies because many whites didn't want to live with black people in the same communities. White landlords also didn't want to rent to blacks.

Decades later, it was the same problem, with many white landlords refusing to rent to black people in areas where they felt blacks were not supposed to live.

That was also still the case with many other landlords, not just white ones, except blacks. Many of them – white and other non-black landlords – even say they don't rent to blacks because black people destroy their property, they are dirty and irresponsible and don't want to pay rent like whites and other tenants do.

It is a racial stereotype against blacks and it's nothing new. Black people expect it to be used against them anytime and it is many times.

The woman who made the remark, "That is how black people are," at the apartment building where we lived, not only reinforced racial stereotypes about blacks; she also showed that it is not just whites who feel that way about black people – there are many people like her who are not white and who are not black who feel the same way and who are just as racist.

She provided empirical evidence and was a specimen of such nonblacks – who include Asians, Hispanics, and even Native Americans among others – who derive pleasure and satisfaction from insulting and demeaning black people in the erroneous belief that by doing so proves they are better than blacks and may even win acceptance by whites as their equals. They think they impress whites when they make such derogatory remarks about blacks.

It is not unusual for such people to spew racist filth even in front of blacks, just like some whites do, and are comfortable, especially among themselves, using the term "nigger" or "niggers" to describe black people even if publicly they say they are liberal and accept blacks as equals.

Such hypocrisy among white liberals still goes on even today; so do racial injustices across the spectrum more than half a century after the civil rights movement which brought about fundamental change in the American society.

Although racism against blacks is almost always seen as a black-white problem, there is another aspect of the problem which is probably overlooked most of the time.

Whites – those who don't like or those who just don't want to associate with blacks not necessarily because they hate or dislike them, as some of them claim – are not the only people blacks have problems with. There are some people of other races or ethnic groups who don't like blacks just like some whites don't. Hispanics, including non-white Hispanics, are a good example of such people.

Even some non-white Hispanics who are black or look just like black people are some of the most hostile towards African Americans. It's probably not many of them but they do exist. When some of them are asked what they are, or if some people think thy are black just like black Americans, they have been known to be very hostile in their response: "I'm no nigger."

One African American I knew very well told me about a black Cuban who was a member of her church in Grand Rapids. At a social gathering organised by their church, some whites called him "black." That was an insult to him. He became very angry and told them, "I'm no nigger."

There are many others who feel the same way. They are Afro-Latinos, racially distinct from other Latinos but sharing the same cultural identity.

They also share geographical and historical bonds as Cubans, Puerto Ricans, Dominicans (from the Dominican Republic not Dominicans from Dominica also known as the Commonwealth of Dominica, a former British colony), also as Mexicans, Hondurans, Nicaraguans, Colombians, Salvadorians or Salvadorans from El Salvador and so on.

When they come to the United States, they maintain their separate and collective identities as Latinos as well as their national identities as Cubans, Mexicans and so forth, distinct from the national identity of Americans even when they become citizens.

Cubans and Puerto Ricans, including Afro-Cubans and Afro-Puerto Ricans – although they are black Latinos or Afro-Latinos – identify themselves with their fellow Latinos (from their homelands who are not black) simply as one and the same people: Cubans or Puerto Ricans, an identification which separates them from black Americans although they are all black.

Puerto Ricans even identify themselves as if they belong to a different country separate from the United States, with their own national identity, although Puerto Rico is not a country but an integral part of the United States.

Even though they come from different countries, they all collectively identify themselves as Latinos, with a common identity as Latinos, although they have differences and even conflicts among themselves along national lines based on their countries of origin.

Black Latinos also have conflicts with their own people – fellow Cubans, fellow Puerto Ricans who are not black – along racial lines because they are not fully accepted by them as their people. Yet they don't identify themselves with black Americans because of their Latino identity. They see themselves, first and last, simply as Latinos like other non-black Latinos.

Even among non-black Latinos, there is animosity; for example, between Puerto Ricans and Mexicans.

I knew some non-black Puerto Ricans in Grand Rapids who said they did not like Mexicans because they thought they were better than they were and called them "niggers."

The Puerto Ricans responded by calling Mexicans "wetbacks," a highly offensive and racist term used to describe Mexicans who enter the United States illegally by swimming across the Rio Grande – which is a part of the US/Mexican border – and getting wet in the river.

One of the Puerto Ricans used to say about Mexicans, "They're too white for me," referring to their attitude towards Puerto Ricans and other people who were not white. And there are such Mexicans, including those who have a brown complexion. I knew some of them. They were brown, yet they called themselves white.

White Hispanics are, on average, at least 65 per cent white. A significant number of them are more white than that. They have a higher percentage of European ancestry, far more than 65 per cent, which partly – if not largely – explains why they legitimately claim to be or identify themselves as white.

Some Hispanics who are even less than half-white, with less than 50 per cent European ancestry, including those who are more black African than anything else also say they are "white."

Their "whiteness" is a mark of distinction and a status symbol because psychologically they want to be and even see themselves as members of a "superior" race to distance themselves from their true identity. They are only deluding themselves. They know they are not white, cannot become white, and will never be white. Yet they continue to be delusional and get extremely offended when they are identified as black or simply as not white.

Most Hispanics in the United States come from Mexico, Puerto Rico (which is a part of the United States), Cuba, El Salvador, the Dominican Republic, Guatemala and Colombia.

Hispanics can be members of any race. But they are

predominantly of Hispanic origin. Their racial – or multiracial – composition is at least 65 per cent European, about 18 per cent Native American, and about 6 per cent black African.

Latinos from Brazil including Afro-Latinos, whose main language is Portuguese, are also loosely classified as Hispanic, a term which denotes ethnicity as an identity more than it does race, comprising diverse groups – or people of different national origin – united by a common Latino culture. There is no Hispanic race. It also includes immigrants from countries in the Americas – the Caribbean and Latin America – which were once ruled by France (Haiti and Martinique) as well as French overseas territories such as French Guiana and Guadeloupe.

Some people from all those countries including French overseas territories in the Americas – who are an integral part of Latino communities in the United States – think they are better than black Americans and other blacks.

Even the Puerto Rican who said about Mexicans "they are too white for me" had a very low opinion of black people. There are other non-black Puerto Ricans who also don't like blacks or think they are better than blacks, an antipathy to black people that is shared by many Mexicans and other non-black Hispanics.

It was the same non-black Hispanic from Puerto Rico who not only hated black Americans but also was notorious for calling Africans "monkeys"; undoubtedly, a characterisation that extended to fellow Puerto Ricans who were black.

There are also some black Puerto Ricans who don't like Africans and African Americans.

The common cultural identity of Hispanics as Latinos – with a Latino culture – sometimes blurs racial distinctions among them and even transcends racial identity among black Latinos who, because of that, identify themselves simply as Latinos, giving primacy to an identity which complicates and even rules out racial identification with black Americans as members of the same race and origin, Africa, except in cases where some Afro-Latinos identify themselves with African Americans as one and the same people.

The emphasis by black Latinos *exclusively* on their Latino identity is deliberately intended to distance themselves from American blacks – as well as black Africans – by claiming they are not black but members of a different "racial" stock, Latino, which is also an ethnic and cultural category.

Black Latinos and white Latinos *don't* belong to the same race although some Afro-Latinos claim they do just to shed their blackness – and African heritage – they should wear with pride like other people do: proud of their origin and identity.

There is visceral hatred of black Americans by some black Hispanics that stems from the perceived inferiority of black people which, because they are black and of African origin themselves, extends to them as well. They therefore do everything they can to distance themselves from that. And in an attempt to do so, some of them use extremely offensive language to describe black Americans and Africans.

Africa, the land of their origin, is a continent of "savages, backward, ignorant, primitive people who run around naked and don't even brush their teeth."

They say they "don't have anything to do with that place and with those people over there."

Even some black Americans and Afro-Caribbeans feel the same way. They say they are not African, they have nothing to do with Africa, and they didn't come from there.

Therefore, the same attitude some black Hispanics have towards Africa is the *same* attitude they have towards black Americans or African Americans since these people "came from over there, their motherland. We did not come from Africa. So, we have nothing to do with them. We are not niggers like them."

Professor Henry Louis Gates, Jr., of Harvard University, in his television series *Black in Latin America on PBS*, met some black Latinos who were ambivalent towards Africa or ashamed of their African origin.

The ambivalence towards Africa among many black Americans, which was more than just an ambivalence but also a longing for reconnection with their motherland, was perhaps best expressed by Countee Cullen when he asked "What is Africa to me?" in his poem "Heritage":

What is Africa to me:

Copper sun or scarlet sea, Jungle star or jungle track,
Strong bronzed men, or regal black Women from whose loins I sprang
When the birds of Eden sang? One three centuries removed
From the scenes his fathers loved,
Spicy grove, cinnamon tree,
What is Africa to me?

The difference between those who are not sure whether or not they should identify with Africa and Cullen as well as others who felt the way he did with regard to Africa is that Cullen, who died in 1946 at the age of 43, wrote the poem in expression of his love for Africa, even if his passionate love for his motherland was somewhat tempered by the negative image of Africa he had known when growing up and during the rest of his short life.

And there are many African Americans today who feel the way he did.

But there is another group of African Americans who are torn apart by two images of Africa. They are attracted by its beauty, and a longing for their roots, reinforcing their romantic image of Africa; yet they are repelled by the harsh realities on the continent: the poverty, the hardship, and even by the primitive condition of the people themselves, so close to them yet so far apart, separated for centuries.

I remember in the early 1980s talking to an African American woman in Grand Rapids, Michigan, who was married to a Nigerian. After she went to Nigeria and came back, she said she couldn't live in Nigeria or anywhere else in Africa because she was not used to the lifestyle and the inconveniences in those countries.

I talked to another one who once lived in Liberia and moved back to Grand Rapids after the 1980 military coup, disgusted with the place because of what the new military rulers did, executing Americo-Liberian leaders and wreaking havoc across Monrovia, the capital.

As an African American, she easily identified with the Americo-Liberians far more than she did with the "natives," if at all. And she did not put in historical perspective the injustices perpetrated by the Americo-Liberians against the indigenous people which prompted a 28-year-old sergeant, Samuel Doe, and 16 of his compatriots from the Liberian army, to seize power after 150 years of Americo- Liberian hegemonic control of the country to the detriment of the native population.

Yet, when she first went to Africa, she had a very romantic view of the motherland as do the majority of black Americans who go there. Compounding the problem was the hardship one experiences living in a poor and underdeveloped Third World country like Liberia.

The same applies to the rest of the countries in Africa, the poorest of the poor – paradoxically in the richest yet poorest continent in the world.

Many African Americans who intended to settle in Africa or live there for an indefinite period of time have been known to turn right back, after only a short stay, vowing never to return except, and that is may be, for short visits. They did not expect to see what they found and saw when they arrived there; a place so attractive, and alluring, with its majestic beauty, yet sometimes so forbidding even to the most hardened soul, except the inordinately ambitious to defy the odds.

That is what prompts many Africans in Africa to ask black Americans: "What did you come here for? We are desperately trying to get out of here and go to America or some other place, and you are dying to come here!" And it is not before long that the harsh reality settles in: "It was a mistake, a big, terrible mistake, to come here. I wish I had known. I would never have left the United States."

But that is only part of the story, in fact not even half of it. A higher percentage of African Americans who go or intend to go to Africa don't have such a negative attitude towards their motherland. Many of them go there, even if not to stay. It is a pilgrimage, a physical and spiritual journey, to the motherland they have never known or seen since they were forcibly uprooted from there and transplanted on American soil permanently. Yet, even some of these returnees also feel out of place when they are in Africa. For cultural and historical reasons, they don't seem to fit in.

In spite of all that, probably an even higher percentage of African Americans, most of whom don't intend to leave the United States and go back to Africa to visit or to stay, have some kind of emotional attachment to the land of their ancestors regardless of how much they hear about that "Dark Continent" as a miserable place: desperately poor, backward, primitive, and intolerable. One clearly sees this in the support African Americans have given to Africa through years, especially during the liberation struggle when the countries of southern Africa were still under white minority rule, and in defending their motherland whenever it is negatively portrayed in the white-dominated media in the United States and elsewhere around the world; and when African interests are ignored by white American leaders and other vested interests.

And they probably could do more if they were not under white control. They operate in a milieu that is not of their making, and in a society whose interests do not necessarily coincide with theirs. White interests are paramount.

Unfortunately, they are despised by some members of other minority groups who themselves face racial discrimination from whites. They include Hispanics, an observation based on my experience and the experience of other blacks in the United States.

Yet, there is also a longing for a spiritual and physical reconnection with Africa even among some black Latinos. But there is also a complete rejection of their roots among some of them probably more than there is such a rejection among African Americans.

It is non-black Hispanics, because of their larger numbers and for racial reasons, who have more confrontations with African Americans and black Africans than black Hispanics do.

Hispanics who are hostile towards blacks – African Americans, Africans and other blacks – are mostly those who are not black even if they look "black" (millions of Indians in India look "black" but they are not black African or people of African origin). Even if they are somewhat brown, but are not of African origin, they feel the same way white Hispanics do about black people. They are also classified as "white." One example illustrates this point.

One non-black brown Hispanic from the Caribbean, in a moment of anger and exasperation, blurted out: "That's how you niggers are."

Yet, through all the years he had been with blacks, interacting with them on regular basis, some of whom were his relatives-in-law, he always identified himself with them – or pretended he did – and said, "We're just niggers," talking about his fellow Hispanics who looked like him. And he collectively identified himself and his fellow Hispanics with blacks saying, "We're all niggers."

Only he knew exactly what he meant when he said

that: "niggers" simply as a term of social identification of blacks and other brown or black-looking nonwhites, hence as an expression of solidarity with black people, or as a term of racial identification, implying brown-looking Hispanics like him also had black African ancestry.

When he said "That's how you niggers are," he was talking about a black man, in front of his wife, in their house! An argument ensued between the two men and that's when he blurted out: "That's how you niggers are.'

If he really believed he was black himself, he would not have said that.

The African American woman whom I knew very well heard the conversation. She was a relative-in-law of the Hispanic man who hurled the racial insult. She was also a friend of the wife of the black man who was insulted in their house; the wife was equally insulted as were all blacks.

I also knew the couple and their children.

The wife told her friend point blank her relative-in-law "is prejudiced."

Her friend did not dispute that. She agreed with her entirely but said she was surprised because all the years she had known him, he identified himself with blacks and often said "we are all niggers."

She had personal experience with racism herself, involving Hispanics who were racist, including her relatives-in-law. Her mother, after she divorced her father, married a Hispanic man from Puerto Rico. She said his relatives including his parents, brothers and sisters and friends were furious; almost all of them were. They were resolutely opposed to the marriage. They did not want him to marry a black woman.

The couple did not have any children during their marriage and stayed married until they died.

The Hispanic husband had a niece who had a black boyfriend. Her family virtually disowned her. Most of her relatives were equally hostile towards her. When she had some children with her black boyfriend, they became even more hostile. Many of them did not even accept the children as their relatives simply because they were half-black.

When the African American woman was growing up in Grand Rapids, she said Hispanic relatives and friends of her Hispanic stepfather were unfriendly towards her and other blacks, except a few of them, very few, who treated her well. Many other Hispanics she met through the years did not like blacks. Even some of the ones who were said to be friendly with blacks were known to be racist.

We also had Hispanic neighbours on the northeast side of Grand Rapids. They lived next door. They did not like black people. They were very hostile towards us. They showed hatred – even just the way they looked at us. We did not even speak to each other.

When their children – not more than six years old – wanted to play with our cat during summer, they pretended they were not against that; they didn't want to look bad stopping their children from paying with our cat.

One day the husband was sitting with her daughter on the sidewalk in front of our residence and theirs when an older black woman, walking on the sidewalk, stopped to say hello to the child, as many older people – especially women – do, greeting and sometimes even playing with children just for a few seconds or so; even when they don't know the children because they see themselves as grandparents to them.

As soon as she did that, leaning towards the child and being friendly with her, the father turned his head away from her and did not even acknowledge her greeting. The black lady just walked away.

Before the Hispanic couple moved into the building next door to ours, two young Hispanic men lived there. They were probably in their late twenties or early thirties. They lived upstairs. Members of a black family rented the apartment downstairs but were later evicted.

When the black tenants were evicted, the two Hispanic men were thrilled. They went downstairs, laughing and spinning around and slapping hands, looking at the apartment from outside – and standing right in front of it – while the landlord and his helpers were inside cleaning up the place. They were glad black people had been evicted.

Soon thereafter, other Hispanics rented the place. They were equally unfriendly to us and to other blacks who came to visit us.

Members of another Hispanic family lived in the same building we did. They had two children, a boy and a girl, about five and six years old. Before the members of the black family next door moved out, their six-year-old child, a girl, tried to play with the Hispanic children. They refused to play with her.

One day, the Hispanic boy told the black girl: "We don't want to play with you." He said it twice and was very loud when he said that, especially the second time.

The black child just stood there, looking at them. The Hispanic boy got even louder, "We don't want to play with you," and was joined by his sister expressing the same sentiment. The black girl finally walked away and went back to her parents' apartment.

Yet the two Hispanic children played with a Hispanic girl who lived in another apartment on the same premises. They played with her all the time. She was also about five or six years old.

It was clear where the hostility of the two Hispanic children came from: their parents who didn't like blacks. The father of the Hispanic children even went to the black family's apartment one afternoon, knocked hard on the door, and told the parents their child was causing trouble and they should keep her away from his family. He was loud enough for anybody in the yard or walking on the street sidewalk to hear what he was saying.

The hostility did not surprise me. It was nothing new. The incident also reminded me of what I heard years before.

In 1980, a white man from Texas – he was probably in his forties, at least, and new to Grand Rapids – was talking to a group of black men and white men (about four blacks including me and two whites) in an informal conversation when the subject of blacks and Hispanics came up.

One of the black men who also came from Texas but lived in Grand Rapids brought up the subject of relations between blacks and Hispanics. The white man said he also came from Texas and knew what was going on down there. He said:

"It's always, *always*, Mexicans who start trouble with blacks. Blacks fight back, though."

It is a nationwide problem, not just between blacks and Mexicans but between blacks and Hispanics in general.

Many years after the white man from Texas talked about the racial problems between blacks and Mexicans, little had changed in terms of relations between the two groups, blacks and Hispanics in general; not all of them but a significant number of them and large enough to justify the conclusion that it was and *still* is a major problem nationwide. And it has been well-documented. One example of that is a study by the Southern Poverty Law Center (SPLC) documented in its report, "Tensions Mounting Between Blacks and Latinos Nationwide."

Blacks and Hispanics have different perspectives even on fundamental issues of common interests.

There is hardly a consensus, let alone agreement, even on some of the most critical matters vital to their collective – or separate – well-being. That is because of the way they see themselves and each other as fundamentally different people in spite of what unites them in their common struggle against those who dominate them.

There is no question that they don't get along well and are on opposite sides, with Hispanics sometimes being virtually in the same camp with whites – and even identifying themselves as white – on various racial matters. For example, during O.J. Simpson's trial, they were on the same side with whites while blacks were virtually alone on the other side.

If there have been any attempts by blacks and Hispanics to form alliances and those attempts have failed, or if no such attempts have been made at all, it is important to ask and answer some questions why that has been the case.

If they don't get along, why don't they? Why do they say they are so different from each other when they face the same social, political and economic problems as minorities, share common goals and employ the same or similar strategies in pursuit of their objectives?

A number of blacks I knew in Grand Rapids said they did not get along with Hispanics because they were racist. They said they got along with whites much better than they did with Hispanics and did not even go to the southwest side of Grand Rapids – on Grandville and other streets in that area – because that was a Hispanic neighbourhood; they did not feel welcome and it was not safe for them to go there.

But there were blacks who went there, including one black man I knew. He used to go to a bar in that area and had Hispanic friends there. And he was not the only one who, now and then, visited the area. I just didn't know any others who did.

What I knew was that the area had a bad reputation among the blacks I knew. I even knew one Hispanic who warned me and another African about the danger we could face from Hispanics. That was in 1980.

He said if a black got involved in a fight with a Hispanic, especially on that side of town, other Hispanics would join the fight to help their fellow Hispanic even if they didn't know him and even if he was at fault and was the one who started the fight. As long as he was fighting a black person, some of his people would help him.

I did not believe all Hispanics were like that; I still don't. Some of them may even call the police or intervene to stop the fight. But what he told us showed just how some of them hated blacks; probably a significant number of them.

Even he himself had his own prejudices against blacks but did not show any of that. He was very careful, and very courteous, in his interactions with blacks; at least from what I knew about him. I knew him for a number of years and he was always very friendly with me and other blacks and liked to socialise with us. There was also a time when he lived with some Africans I knew in Grand Rapids. They rented a house together.

One afternoon during summer in 1979, I went to visit them. It was a very warm day and the door was open. When I knocked on the door and walked in, I saw the Hispanic man sitting at a table with a white man. They were drinking some beer. Before I could even finish saying "Hello," the Hispanic man abruptly interrupted me, as if he didn't even know me in front of the white man, and pointed upstairs saying, "They're upstairs."

He didn't want to introduce me to the white man and didn't want him to know I knew him. He obviously wanted the white man to believe that I did not go there to visit him and his African roommates – I was there to visit *only* them, my fellow Africans, and they were upstairs; and they were, and I went up there.

Yet this was the same man who liked to mingle and socialise with us and other blacks. He had never shown any signs of prejudice against us in the past – let alone engage in a public display of racial animus.

All those incidents demonstrate one simple truth: There is prejudice against blacks even by some people who are victims of racism themselves in a predominantly white society. And they don't care about blacks anymore than many whites do. Their attitude is: "Yes, white people think

they are better than we are. But we are better than blacks."
And black people know that from experience when they
interact with Hispanics and other nonwhites.

Some blacks even reciprocate such hostility directed
against them simply because they are black and despised
for no other reason than that.

I witnessed an incident during which one black man
who was my neighbour expressed his distrust of, and
disgust with, of Hispanics.

He came to visit me one day in 1980 and when he saw
the Hispanic man – I described above – in my house who
was also visiting me, his attitude changed. There were two
other blacks in my house on that day. We were all sitting
down and drinking some beer when, in a casual manner
but smirking at the same time, he asked: "What's he doing
here?"

The other two blacks just smiled, somewhat, to lighten
up the occasion and avoid embarrassing the Hispanic
visitor. I told my neighbour without hesitation that the
Hispanic man was visiting me just as he and the other two
blacks were.

The Hispanic visitor got the message. He already knew
about the tense – sometimes outright hostile – relationship
between some blacks and some Hispanics. And there are
some blacks, not just my visitor, who don't hesitate to
respond in kind when Hispanics are hostile towards them:
"If we are not welcome in your neighbourhood, you are
not welcome in ours (the inner city, or the ghetto, the black
homeland). And if you don't like us, we don't like you
either. So stay away from us and we're going to stay away
from you."

That was my neighbour's attitude. And it is a collective
sentiment expressed by different blacks at different times
even though, in general, blacks and Hispanics often get
along well as much as they do with whites and other
people. But there are tense moments between the two just
as there are with other people for racial reasons.

Yet, from my own experience through the years since my student days in Detroit in the early seventies, I have not faced overt racism from most whites with whom I have interacted.

Most of them have been cordial, friendly, and courteous – even if some of them were covertly racist.

In most cases, racism is not overtly expressed. It has been transmuted from raw-naked bigotry into refined non-acceptance of blacks by simply ignoring them, yet acknowledging their presence as fellow human beings while harbouring racist beliefs that "they are still not as good as we are." It enables white racists to say this is post-racial America – we now live in a colour-blind society.

That is a polite form of racism among many whites which is sharply contrasted with the crude manners of some bigots who spew racist filth against blacks and other nonwhites. And it is even more corrosive in the long-term because it is hard to detect and unmask when some of the people who practise it are some of the most respected and enlightened members of society including ministers.

And as a black person, I know it is not just a black-white problem. It is also a black-Hispanic problem and a problem with members of other races who also despise and don't like black people. In the American context, Hispanics stand out because they are the second-largest "racial" or ethnic category after whites black people have to deal with.

I don't know what my experience would have been had I interacted with many Hispanics. I probably would have had the same experience blacks I knew had when they said many Hispanics did not like black people. And that is probably true. There are also many whites who don't like blacks.

It is impossible to know how many there are, in every racial category, but there are such people, even among blacks, who don't like people of other races for different reasons.

Some racists are even blunt about their feelings towards blacks even when they are in front of many people. It happened to me at a predominantly white bar in in Grand Rapids in 1981.

A white band was playing there one night and the band leader asked members of the audience what song they wanted to be played. The band played all the songs white patrons asked them to play. When I mentioned one song – I was sitting near the front – he abruptly responded, "We don't know that song," and shook his head, looking at me straight face. He lied. It was a very popular song and was played on the radio all the time.

He just wanted to make a point that as a black person, I was not welcome there. There were very few other blacks. I would not have gone to the bar if it was all-white – I would have known there had to be a good reason why black people did not want to go there; but it was not.

All these racial incidents – not only do they have a cumulative impact on blacks; they define the status of black people in the United States and show how members of other races see them.

Yes, other nonwhites are also victims of racism. But it is blacks, more than members of any other racial or ethnic group, who face rejection and isolation even by other nonwhites. It is a rejection and isolation that also helps to reinforce and solidify black identity and solidarity which is sometimes misconstrued as a form of racism by black people because they "isolate" themselves from members of other racial groups, while the reverse is the case.

I was also a victim of racial profiling by the police in Grand Rapids years ago.

It is a problem inextricably linked with the nation's history and contemporary realities in terms of race relations. Stereotypes abound, including the belief that young black men commit most of the crimes in the United States, a racial stereotype that has been used to justify racial profiling and even police brutality against blacks:

young black men being stopped by the police at will for being crime suspects and very often manhandled by white police officers.

But just being black is enough to be stopped by the police regardless of age or gender although a disproportionately large number of young black men across the nation are routinely stopped and frisked by the police ostensibly to stop crime. It is a highly contentious subject whose volatile nature has fuelled debate on relations between blacks – as well as Hispanics – and the police.

One day, in the summer of 1983, I was on my way to a friend's house in an area that is near downtown Grand Rapids. It was just before sunset and I was walking, enjoying the weather.

A police car was parked on the other side of the street. A white police officer sitting in the car saw me and said, loudly, "Hey, come here."

As I approached the car and was only a few feet away from him, he asked me: "Is that a gun in your pocket?"
I said, "No, it's my hair pick." It had a wooden handle shaped like the map of Africa.

"Let me see it," he said.

I took it out of my front pocket and he looked at it. I was very careful not to point it at him and held it pointing downwards.

Fully aware of who and what I was as a black man, facing a white police officer, I did not want to give him any kind of excuse, not the slightest excuse – none whatsoever – for him to pull out his gun on me. He could have said I pointed a gun at him and that was why he shot me.

Next, he asked me, "Where are you going?"
I said, "To my friend's house."
"Where does he live?"
I told him where my friend lived.
He finally said, "OK," and I left.

When he first called me, he did not even see anything bulging in my pocket which he could have thought was a gun. He could not have seen it because I was many feet away from him, on the other side of the street, and my hair pick was in my front pocket where it fit in perfectly without bulging or protruding like a pistol. It was a flat hair pick.

Had it been in my back pocket, I might have thought he probably saw something bulging or sticking out of my pocket. But even it did, it would not have looked like a gun. It would have been the metal hair picks sticking out while the handle, shaped like an African map, was deep inside my pocket without bulging since it was flat as most hair picks – almost all of them – are.

There was only one reason why he focused his attention on me. I was a young black man, "just another nigger up to no good."

I was not offended because that was something I expected to happen to me as a black man. I knew whites are not randomly and routinely stopped and searched by police officers the way black people, especially young black men, are. And I knew it was wrong for the police officer to stop me simply because I was black.

My main concern, not fear, was what he was thinking when he called me. As a white officer, seeing a black man walking on the street, he may have thought I was "just another black thug from the ghetto, up to no good."

I lived in the ghetto even though the policeman did not know that. I never told him where I lived and he never asked me about that. But he probably assumed that was where I lived, in the ghetto, home to most blacks in Grand Rapids just like other blacks across the nation who also live in the inner city.

But even if I told him I did not live in the ghetto, and he believed me, it would have made absolutely no difference to him in terms of perception of what type of person I was: first and foremost, as a black man suspected of breaking the law, carrying a concealed weapon, a pistol in my pocket, without a permit. He may have seen me as a potential criminal or just a criminal. That is the first thing that is on the mind of many white police officers when they see and stop black men in the streets.

The perception is reinforced by the racial stereotype many whites have about blacks. They say we all look alike. They even probably believe we all think the same way, as a monolithic whole, usually in a negative way. They think many of us think about committing crime.

This perception and misconception and denigration of black people, also applies to blacks who live outside the ghetto including those who live in integrated neighbourhoods and even in affluent areas.

Many whites say we are all the same in terms of mentality, conduct and way of life, a belief that validates in their minds the saying which is loaded with racist connotations: "You can take a Negro out of the ghetto but you can't take the ghetto out of the Negro."

Therefore, to the white police officer who stopped me for no reason besides racial profiling, I was "just another nigger." "You know how niggers are. Committing *all that crime*."

That is the attitude of many of them. In fact, that's why he stopped me and asked me where I was going and if what I had in my pocket was a gun.

The list goes on and on – about the things they say about black people. Many other whites, not just white police officers, have the same attitude towards blacks.

Had I been a white man, just walking, the police officer would probably not even have kept on looking at me – let alone stop me and ask me to go to him. The colour of my skin triggered something in his mind right away.

To many white policemen, it infuriates them and has their adrenaline flowing, ready to pull the trigger – just at the sight of a black man – and do the unthinkable.

I was black, therefore suspected of doing or getting

ready to do something wrong, including having a pistol in my pocket to try and rob someone.

Many young black men are prime suspects and are known to "carry guns." Whites including police officers really believe that.

I knew there are things in life I have to be prepared to face as a black person in a predominantly white society without anger or animosity and simply go on with my life even if what I say may be misconstrued as condoning racism. It is simply a fact of life and we have to live with it. And that includes racial profiling by the police, by white business owners and employees in stores and shops who constantly watch or follow black customers around, men and women, young and old, because they believe if you are black, you are going to steal something.

Racial profiling by the police in Grand Rapids, as in other parts of the country, has sparked outrage from blacks, Hispanics and even from some whites and has sometimes been the subject of discussion at public meetings and forums.

There is no true racial equality. It is a myth. Those who are in control don't want other people to have equality. The best that can be expected is contain racism and racial injustice and minimise its impact on its victims. It can't be eradicated when those who control and dominate society want to perpetuate it for their own benefit at the expense of their victims.

Many whites *don't* want to end racism and racial injustice because it benefits them socially, politically, economically – and even psychologically, deriving pleasure from the fact that they are on top simply because they are white and their people – fellow whites – are in control.

Even some of the poorest and least successful whites think they are better than all blacks including the most successful.

"My people are on top, therefore I am on top."

"What do you think about successful blacks?"

"They are still black, aren't they?"

"What do you think about a black doctor, a black lawyer, a black professor, a black scientist, a black engineer, a black mayor, a black congressman?"

"He's just another nigger to me."

That's their logic. And it pervades society.

The majority of the white racists don't use such crude language in public although many of them probably do so in the privacy of their homes and among their friends and relatives. But they are just as racist. They are the polite racists, with refined manners, your good neighbours next door, and "true" Christians. And they constitute the vast majority of the white racists in the United States.

They are also the biggest problem in the struggle for racial equality and justice because of their numerical preponderance among racists and because of their unwillingness to bring about fundamental change in society in the quest for equality among the people all races. They are a part of the silent majority whose silence is tantamount to condoning racism.

Many of them admit racism still is a major problem in the United States. But they are reluctant or don't want to do anything about it. They say they are not racist. And they are responsible for the wide gulf in race relations that exists in the United States today, especially between blacks and whites.

The racial divisions which became so pronounced during Trump's presidency only confirmed the existence of a problem that was already there and which has existed for a long time even before Trump was born and for a much longer period even before then.

It is a problem that has plagued the nation since its founding, a nation founded on slavery, a system that was inherently racist despite its economic motivations as the main driving force behind it.

Yes, Trump made the problem worse. But he did not

start it. The race problem will continue to haunt the nation indefinitely.

Yes, perpetrators of this evil should be punished. But the problem will always exist because of man's inherent capacity for evil, motivated by his base instincts more than anything else, despite his equally inherent capacity to do good.

That is exactly what it means when people say we have made some progress, or a lot of progress, in the quest for racial equality but we still have a long way to go. They are going to say the same thing fifty years from now, and a hundred years from now, till kingdom come.

I had another encounter with the police, similar to the one I described earlier, almost eleven years before then. That was in November 1972 in New York City. I was there for about two months.

I was at LaGuardia airport getting ready to catch a plane on a flight to Washington. D.C., to visit some of my friends from Trinidad whom I mentioned earlier.

I was waiting in line getting ready to board the plane when a uniformed police officer asked me to step aside. He was white. He asked me who I was, where I was going, and where I lived. As he was asking me those questions, he was also busy frisking me, patting me up and down. He also checked my pockets. I showed him my Tanzanian passport with a valid visa.

I told him I was staying with a relative in Manhattan. I also gave him the address, 16th Floor, Sutton House, 415 East 52nd. I showed him a card my relative had given me which he said I should show to the authorities, including the police, in case I had some problems with them. He said: "Tell them to call me." He also signed the card.

He said as long as I stayed with him, I was not supposed to be arrested because he was a diplomat – he worked at the Tanzania Mission to the UN – and any relative living with him was also covered and protected under diplomatic immunity.

I knew about diplomatic immunity but did not know the exact circumstances under which it is invoked – besides knowing that immediate family members of diplomats, spouses and children, are protected. I did not know their relatives were also protected if they lived or stayed with them.

The Tanzania Mission to the UN was on East 42nd within walking distance from where I stayed. I went there quite often to read Tanzanian newspapers, so far away from home.

I told the police officer who my relative was and where he worked. He looked at the card and and looked at me and let me go. He was very hostile towards me. I don't know what would have happened to me had he not found out I was staying with a relative who was a diplomat.

That may have helped me. But it also showed glaring inequalities in society, any society, when some people are treated better than others – tragic cases of social injustice. Had another African, or even a black American, been in the same situation, without any connection to some influential or powerful people, he could have been arrested and locked up on mere suspicion of being a terrorist or plane hijacker.

What the white policeman did to me was clearly a case of racial profiling. But something else also stood out about me.

I was in African attire, a dashiki and a Sekou Toure hat – that's what it was called and was worn by President Sekou Toure of Guinea and was very popular among some Africans during those days – an appearance which triggered something in the policeman's mind.

He obviously thought he was dealing with a black militant. That was also in the same year (earlier in July) when some Black Panther Party members were accused of hijacking a plane to Algeria and doing other things the government did not like.

Some Black Panther Party members and other black

militants also wore dashikis and other African clothes including African hats.

After I was singled out, I was fully convinced it had to do with that. The police officer may have thought I was a Black Panther or some other kind of black militant getting ready to hijack the plane.

There were other blacks, men and women, in front of me and behind me, who were not asked to step aside to be frisked by the white policeman.

I remember one of them who was just a little farther behind me and how he looked at me when I was being patted up and down by the police officer who asked me to put my hands up.

He probably knew why. He was black himself. I doubt he thought race was not a factor in my being pulled aside and frisked by the policeman. He may have thought the same way about my very un-American attire which gave me the appearance of a black militant.

The difference was that had a white man been dressed the same way, his African clothes would probably not have raised any suspicion in the white policeman's mind that he was a potential terrorist or airplane hijacker.

Regardless of how one looks at it, there is no question that my identity as a black man played a major role in my being singled out, in addition to my attire which to the police officer was very un-American and very militant cast in the Black Panther mould.

My experience with the policeman in New York, and with another one in Grand Rapids almost eleven years later, was only a small part of the cumulative experience of black people – the daily slights and insults and countless acts of overt and covert as well as brutal racism – which I became even more familiar with through the decades because of my identity as a black person and living my life as a black man in a multiracial society dominated by whites in all areas.

There are numerous cases of racism spanning the entire

socio-political and economic spectrum. But some of them stand out more than others do because of their egregious nature.

Besides racial injustices under the judicial system including racial profiling and police bias against blacks, discrimination in housing is one of the most persistent problems blacks face across the nation. It is one of the pillars of racism in the United States.

Discrimination in housing is so serious that it can even be dangerous for blacks to move into some areas which are considered to be "white." It is a nationwide problem and Grand Rapids is no exception, although the city has reached a level of integration that was unheard of in the seventies and even in the eighties.

When I moved from Detroit to Grand Rapids in 1976, a fundamental change had taken place in the city only six years before in terms of housing. Blacks had been virtually confined to a certain area, the ghetto in the inner city, clearly demarcated by major streets as the boundaries between black and white areas. I lived in that area for many years.

As a black man, segregation played a major role in my choice of where I could live in the city. Even if I had arrived six years before, in 1970, I probably would have made the same decision and would have chosen to live in the inner city where I would have felt I would be more welcome than I would be in white neighbourhoods:

"Segregation in the city of Grand Rapids is nothing new to long-time residents who faced years of redlining. It was not until 1970 that black residents were able to purchase homes outside of Hall Street on the south, Cherry Street on the north, Fuller on the east, and the river to the west....

Per the Home Owners' Loan Corporation maps from 1937, Black Americans in Grand Rapids lived in areas labeled as hazardous. The Home Owners' Loan

Corporation is a corporation established in 1933 under the Home Owners' Loan Corporation Act passed by President Franklin D. Roosevelt. The purpose of this act was to help refinance home mortgages who were at risk or in foreclosure.

During this time, The Federal Housing Administration worked with the HOLC to help grade neighborhoods from green to red. The areas where Black Americans lived were consistently labeled as red. A 'green' grading was considered the best grading and was given primarily to white resident occupied neighborhoods....

Access to high grade housing and economic prosperity has been consistently denied to communities of color in the city. According to U.S. Census data, 26 percent of residents in Grand Rapids are living in poverty. Out of those unemployed in Kent County, residents of color make up 94 percent, according to the 2015 report from the Michigan Department of Civil Rights, 'The High Cost of Disparities.'" – (Michelle Jokisch Polo, "Grandville Avenue: A Neighborhood Confronted with a History of Redlining and Segregation," *On The Ground*, Grand Rapids, Michigan, November 2017).

I lived in the black area described above for almost sixteen years before moving to a sparsely integrated neighborhood on the northeast side of the city where I also lived for many years.

Things have changed, gradually, through the years although not as much as they should and could have. Not only do blacks now live in all parts of the city – they have even spread out into others areas such as Kentwood, Wyoming, and even Grandville, which are outside Grand Rapids but still an integral part of the metropolitan area.

It is a step towards integration and an achievement that must be acknowledged. It has been reported that 60 per cent of blacks in the Grand Rapids metropolitan area now live outside the ghetto, especially in Kenwtood and

Wyoming more than in any other suburban areas.

There are still many blacks in the inner city. But those who are stuck in the ghetto are mostly the poor.

What is obscured by those statistics, however impressive and glowing they may be in terms of racial integration in the suburbs of Grand Rapids, is the existence of racism even in those areas.

Racism follows you wherever you go if you are black or if you are Hispanic or some other nonwhite – regardless of where you live. Simply because an area is integrated does not mean it is not plagued by racism. The only difference is that in some of those areas, racism may be more covert than overt. That is also the main reason many people don't talk about it and don't even want to talk about it.

All those are serious issues that need to be addressed by the members of all races, not just by blacks, Hispanics and other victims of injustice include poor whites. And just because integrated housing is a relatively common feature of life in the Grand Rapids metropolitan area does not mean residential or housing segregation is no longer a problem; it still is.

And there have been attempts through the years to address racism even in suburban areas such as Kentwood and Wyoming which are predominantly white and where a significant number of blacks live as never before. Dialogue across racial lines is critical to finding solutions to racial problems. It enables people to face those problems and engage in fruitful conversations.

Such conversations can facilitate racial understanding between groups and individuals even in areas where the people are very hostile towards blacks and other nonwhites – but *only if* the people involved are *genuinely* interested in achieving racial harmony. Otherwise it is no more than empty rhetoric.

There is no question that progress has been made even in places such as northwest Grand Rapids where there are some blacks who live there although it is still not a hospitable place for nonwhites, especially black people, like some parts of the city are.

When I moved from Detroit to Grand Rapids and had been in the city for about six years after attending Aquinas College, I wanted to rent an apartment on the northwest side. I did not know the area was dangerous for blacks.

One African American warned me, "Don't you know they don't like blacks on the northwest side? Don't go there." I didn't know, of course, and heeded his advice.

Later, I found out the northwest side of Grand Rapids had been prohibited territory for decades; blacks dare not go there.

A few years later, another African American told me about the terror she experienced when she and her son, a teenager, rented a house on that side of town in March 1980. They did not last long. They were there for only some months.

When they first moved in, she heard some whites who saw them at the house they were renting say: "We didn't know any niggers lived over here."

They moved into the "wrong" area.

One day, an older white lady who was in her late eighties, almost 90 years old, was walking past the house the black woman was renting on the northwest side of Grand Rapids. She stopped to talk to her and told her she was her neighbour and lived right next door to her. She was very friendly.

She told the black woman that she had lived on that side of town for thirty years and in all those years she had never seen any blacks living there. She told her she was the first black person she had seen who had moved into that area and wished her the best because it was not safe for blacks to live there.

She talked to her often and did not show any hostility towards her and her son and said she was a Christian.

The white neighbours on the other side of the house the

black woman was renting were extremely hostile towards her and her son. Their wives and girlfriends were equally hostile.

One day, some of them poured some beer on the car of the black woman's mother when she went to visit her and her grandson. They didn't say anything to them and could have been attacked had they complained about the incident.

The black woman's mother was a missionary worker of the Seventh-Day Adventist church but never ventured into that area to do missionary work. Her daughter was also a missionary worker and a member of the same church.

The white neighbours and their friends often yelled, "niggers" at the black woman and her son whenever they saw them and used profanities threatening them.

One night, while yelling "niggers" outside the house, one of them shot into the kitchen. The black woman was in there and the bullet barely missed her.

Her son had a white friend who was his classmate. Whenever he went to visit them, whites in the area would yell at him, calling him "Nigger lover," and chased him a number of times, threatening him with physical harm.

Across the street was a white couple who had a dog. The dog, a collie, was very friendly.

One day, the black woman and her son were walking near the house on their way to a grocery store when the dog went towards them, wagging its tail. The black woman was getting ready to pat the dog when the white owner yelled, "Don't you touch the dog. Come back Skipper!" That was the dog's name.

The black woman and her son kept on walking. They didn't say anything to the dog's owner when he yelled at them.

There was also a white girl who lived very close to the house the black woman was renting. She was about 13 years old.

She went to their house one day in June 1980 when the

black woman had a birthday party for her son. It was his 16th birthday.

The black woman invited some children from her church to join her son in celebrating his birthday. Some of them came with their friends from other churches. The son also invited some of his schoolmates.

There were members of all races at the party. They were outside the house enjoying themselves.

When the 13-year-old white girl saw them, she wanted to join them. She went to the house; it was only a few yards away from where she lived with her parents.

She was very friendly. But her parents were extremely hostile towards blacks. She told the black woman white people in that part of Grand Rapids did not like blacks. She heard it all the time from her parents and other whites in the area.

When her father found out she went to the black woman's house, mingling with blacks, he was furious. He went to get her. He didn't care other white children, mostly teenagers, were also at the party. What infuriated him was her daughter's decision to go to a black family's house and socialise with them.

On the way back to his house with his daughter, he gave her a thorough beating and yelled at her, "Don't you ever go to that house and talk to those niggers again."

He was loud enough for everybody nearby to hear that. The black woman and her son as well as other children who were there also heard that.

He beat up his daughter so bad that the black woman and her son and other people thought he was going to kill her.

Someone called the police and several police cars went there.

The father hated black people so much that he was ready to go to jail and even to prison for beating up his daughter simply because she was friendly with blacks.

The African American woman had a friend, also black,

whose husband was called a "nigger" by some whites on the northwest side. The black man was there with his wife. When they called him "nigger," he looked at them and told them, "I'll show you what kind of nigger I am."

They knew he wasn't playing and tried to get away in a car. He went after them in his truck and got involved in a high-speed chase trying to catch them. But they got away. His wife was in the truck with him and told her friend she would never forget that day. She said her husband drove so fast, and he was so angry, that she feared they would end up in a very bad accident. Unfortunately, they did not.

Her husband was one of those blacks who simply don't tolerate racial insults and are ready to fight anybody even if they end up in jail – even in prison – because of that.

The black woman's son had a white teacher who lived in that part of Grand Rapids. He told the black woman he knew of only two black families who once rented houses on the northwest side sometime ago but did not last long; they were terrorised by white racists who even set the garage of one of the houses on fire and forced them to move out of there.

The black woman and her son were also terrorised by some whites and forced to move out of the northwest side. Their landlord was the ring leader, one of his sons, who had a black girlfriend, told the victims.

When they first moved there, the landlord himself warned them to stay off the streets for their own safety. He said they would be killed by racist whites on that side of town if they were seen walking on the streets and should stay "invisible" as much as they could.

He went on to say it was safe for whites to be in the ghetto and other black communities than it was for blacks to be in white neighbourhoods even if they were just passing through.

His wife was with him when he was saying all that. She was very angry and visibly so. Just like her husband, she did not want blacks to rent the house or live anywhere on the northwest side.

The black woman's mother was also there when the landlord was giving all those warnings and told her daughter she noticed, just like her daughter did, how angry the landlord's wife was. She showed a lot of hate and did not even try to disguise it. She wanted them to know she hated blacks and did not want them there.

The only difference between her and her husband was that her husband was "friendly" and smiling when he talked to the black woman who rented his house, pretending he was concerned about her safety and well-being, and her son's, and had to warn them about the danger they were in when they moved to the northwest side – which was literally off bounds for blacks.

The landlord's son also said it was his father who rigged the stove in the house the African American woman and her son were renting. He told her his father rigged the stove to produce poisonous gas including carbon monoxide in order to kill her and her son.

Whenever the landlord went to the house supposedly to do some maintenance work, the black woman renting the house told him there was soot on the wall which she had to wipe off everyday; there was something wrong with the stove, she said. It was a serious complaint but the landlord dismissed it lightly saying there was nothing to worry about – it was just an old stove.

When they went to see the doctor because their condition was deteriorating, he told them it was because of carbon monoxide poisoning. Police detectives got involved in the case. They went to the house she was renting from the racist landlord and blamed her. "Get your coat." It was during winter and they were ready to take her to jail.

They accused her of trying to kill her son by poisoning him. They were getting ready to arrest her but the doctor intervened and told them the poisonous gas was carbon monoxide coming from the stove.

It was the same landlord, who was trying to kill them, who first warned them when they rented the house about the danger they were facing as blacks on that side of town. He said he was a Christian and did not want anything to happen to them; they should be very careful and should not mingle or even associate with the people in that area. They should stay in the house or on their premises unless they had to go somewhere.

Yet, his son said it was his father and his mother who organised block meetings in the area to keep blacks out of there. Block meetings were attended by residents – all white – who lived on the streets in the area, with each block composed of several or many houses on a street.

The son knew about the meetings and who attended those meetings organised and led by his parents. He had nothing to do with them. And he strongly disagreed with his parents on that.

And when his father found out his son had a black girlfriend, and even lived with her, in the ghetto, he was furious. He stopped supporting him financially and virtually disowned him.

His father vowed he would take him out of his will if he continued to have a black girlfriend and black friends and would leave him nothing to inherit. He said the same thing to his other son who also had black friends.

The son who lived with his black girlfriend said his mother was equally racist but not overtly like his father; that was the only difference.

He also told the African American woman that his father and other whites had done a lot of bad things to black people on the northwest side of Grand Rapids and elsewhere and she and her son could even get killed if they continued to live there. They were in extreme danger.

He said his father and his gang would set the house on fire and burn it down or shoot them if they came out running.

He advised her to go to the the civil rights commission

and tell them about the problems she and her son were having to see if something could be done – which was sheer wishful thinking – otherwise the racial threats and harassment would continue and their lives would be in extreme danger.

The civil rights commission would not have been able to protect them or provide them with security round-the-clock.

Several times, she and her son saw some whites around the house at night, knocking on doors and windows, threatening them and telling them black people – niggers – were not welcome on that side of Grand Rapids; the northwest side was for whites *only*.

The landlord's son told the African American woman and her son that he knew about all that and that his father was not only the leader of the gang of racists who were threatening and harassing them; he was with them on the premises at night.

The African American woman had an uncle who was almost all-white. He looked white and said he was one-eighth black. He told her she should *never* have moved to the northwest side – they don't like people.

When they first moved there, they were warned by more than one person on that side: "Stay off the streets. Otherwise you will be attacked."

One of the people who warned them, the landlord, even patted them on the back saying he was different and would never do such a thing to them.

It was time to go.

They moved back to the inner city, a euphemism for "ghetto," which was black.

In addition to being falsely accused of trying to kill her own son by poisoning her, the African American woman had earlier faced the same problem with the police; accused of committing crime she did not commit.

A few years before then, police detectives accused her of being a part of group of burglars who broke into the building where she worked alone at night.

She said she always saw some cars in the parking lot – when none was supposed to be there – and wondered what was going on. She saw several young white men sitting in the cars and looking at her. She said she would call the police now and then but when the police came, they found nothing on them and no reason to arrest them.

One night, after she was gone, they broke into the building, also broke into a safe, and stole a lot of money. She had told the business owners several times about the suspicious individuals who were sitting in the cars in the parking lot every night and thought they probably intended to break into the building. When they did, detectives went there and were ready to arrest her for conspiring with the burglars to commit the crime.

She did not conspire with the burglars to help them break into the building.

Even the business owners intervened on her behalf and told the police that she had warned them many times about the suspicious individuals she saw every night sitting in cars in the parking lot.

The detectives were ready to arrest her, not because she helped the burglars to break into the building; they were going to arrest her simply because she was black. They did not trust her and did not believe she was telling them the truth because of the racial stereotype about black people being liars and criminals; it was nothing but racism which motivated them in their attempt to arrest her and even charge her for a crime she did not commit.

The police detectives, all of whom were white, finally relented after the business owners intervened. They told her she won't be so lucky next time; the burglars were professionals, they left no fingerprints and they could come back to rob the place again and they could kill her.

All the time when she was being interrogated at her job, she told the detectives she had nothing to do with the break-in and had warned the owners about a potential burglary but had not been taken seriously until they conceded after the break-in that she had been right all the time and they should have paid attention to her warnings. The detectives were not impressed.

Without the intervention by the owners, she would have been arrested and would probably have been sentenced to a long prison term based on fabricated evidence by the police.

Even black women face such problems, although black men, especially young black men, are accused of committing crime, often falsely, and arrested more than black women are.

Not long after that, she had another encounter with the police. Coincidentally, when that happened to her, she was living on the same street in the Baxter Community where I once lived for a number of years.

She had an encounter with police in 1987, a few years after I moved from there.

The police went to her house one night, around 2 AM, and falsely claimed they had seen a young black man who had stolen a car go into her house. Three white police officers, two men and one woman, were involved in this incident. They parked their police cars on the same street where she lived with her son and very close to the house.

The police did that, now and then, trying to catch criminals in the ghetto. And they sometimes falsely accused blacks – who lived there and even those who were just passing through – of committing crime, especially robberies, break-ins, and drug trafficking.

She was asleep when they went to her house and knocked on the door. When she opened the door, they asked her why she took so long to answer. She said she was asleep.

They asked her about the young man they claimed had stolen a car and gone into her house. She told them no young black man had gone to her house and sought refuge after stealing a car – let alone let him in.

She told them they could search the house. As soon as they walked in, they saw a white girl, 18 years old, in the living room, lying on the couch. The female police officer went into another room with the African American woman who was renting the house to talk to her.

When they were in the room, the black woman heard the two male police officers talking to the white girl in the other room and asking her: "What are you doing with these niggers?" They said she was kidnapped by them.

She told them she was not kidnapped. She said they were her friends and defended them.

The two white police officers were angry the white girl was staying with blacks, in the ghetto, and defending them. After they left, she told the black woman: "The cops are prejudiced."

She went to stay with the black woman because she had nowhere to go. The two met at work, where they worked together, and the African American woman offered her a place to stay when she told her she had nowhere to live.

To the racist police officers, that was still not a good reason for her to live "with niggers" – whom they had also falsely accused of harbouring a fugitive who had stolen a car and was running away from the law.

There was no such fugitive. And no car had been stolen in the area.

But when you are black, dealing with racist cops, expect anything. Anything is possible including getting killed by them for "threatening them and pointing a gun at them" even if you did not threaten them with anything, let alone point a gun at them.

Many blacks, especially black men, have been killed, and continue to be killed, by white police officers for no other reason than that: for being black.

It could have happened to me. I could have been shot when I had an encounter with the white police officer who stopped me in1983 had he felt "threatened" by me for pulling out "a gun" – my hair pick – on him when he asked me what did I have in my pocket, a gun?

Just finding a place to live is hard enough when you are black, let alone being harassed and threatened by police officers who could end up taking your life for nothing.

The African American woman whom I knew for years also had other encounters with racists when she moved from the northwest side of Grand Rapids to another part of the city.

She fled from racists, only to run into more racists.

In September 1983, she found an apartment in a building downtown and decided to rent it. After she moved in with her son, she found out the building was "exclusively" for whites.

The few blacks, only a handful who had moved in there at different times before she did, were forced to move out after being threatened by whites living in the building; the whites went in groups, threatening them.

She was threatened the same way and almost got killed when they broke down the door of her apartment.

One evening – it was still daylight – a group of whites went to her apartment to attack them. One of them kicked the apartment's door so hard that it came off the hinges.

She and her son, who was 19 years old then, screamed for some help and banged on the wall of an apartment next to theirs that was rented by a black woman who was old enough to be her mother. She heard them and came out with her pistol. She was not afraid of anyone – that's just how she was – and was ready to fight them. They ran away when they saw she had a gun.

The black woman and her son called the police. When the police came, the white man who was the ringleader of the racist gang and who was the one who kicked the door was staggering, pretending to be drunk. He fell down and lay on his back, yelling, "Yes, I kicked those niggers' door."

The police said they got the people who were

responsible for the attack. One of them even tried to impress the victims when he told them, "We got our man," in pointed reference to the man who kicked their door.

Yet they did nothing to help her and her son. No one was arrested – let alone prosecuted. Instead, they gave the black woman a card and told her to call them if she had any more trouble with some of the people in the building.

She had been told by one black man who lived in the building when she first moved in: "They don't want any niggers in here."

He worked for them to keep other blacks out of the building. He did whatever they told him to do.

The black woman with the pistol – mentioned above – told the black woman whose door was kicked off the hinges: "He's too Southern for me."

She came from the South herself but was brought up in the North.

The black man who worked for the racists in the building also came from the South and was brought up down there. He told the two black women: "I am the see-after," working for the racists in the building – whatever that expression, "I am the see-after," meant in standard English. He was very ignorant.

On another occasion, the older black woman told him directly: "Do you think these white folks care about you? You're a fool."

The younger black woman and her son – together with her mother – went to the police station, downtown Grand Rapids, to talk to a black female detective who was well-connected to the ghetto and did a lot of police work in the inner city where she also lived. When she told her what happened, that she and her son almost got killed by some whites in the apartment building where they were living, the detective said emphatically: "They are not going to arrest white people for you. They don't even want *me* here."

She meant that the white police officers and detectives

did not want her working at the police department. Even the African American woman and her mother noticed that when they were sitting in front of the black detective. They saw how the other detectives – all white – were looking at her. They were very unfriendly.

When they were still at the police station, the manager of the apartment building where the black woman and her son were being terrorised called the black detective. The manager was a white woman. She knew the black detective was handling the case involving the black woman and her son.

The building manager told the detective that the black woman's son was tearing up wallpaper in the apartment building and had tenants – white tenants – complaining about it.

The black detective was infuriated by what the apartment building manager said. She told her: "You are a liar. Ms (name withheld) son can't be tearing up wallpaper in the apartment building. She's sitting right here, in front of me, with her son. He can't be tearing up wallpaper in the building."

She slammed the phone so hard that it seemed she broke it. She was so angry.

Sometime later, the African American female victim of racist attacks went to see a white civil rights lawyer in order to get some help. The lawyer told her he knew about the building. He said they wanted the whole building to be only for white tenants. He also told her he would take the case but warned her there would be consequences for doing that because that would be going against "some big people."

He also told her she could pursue the matter in another way by going to the civil rights commission but if she did so and ended up on television, she could be in extreme danger and face retaliation. "They will go after your son first," he said.

She didn't go any further. She moved out of the

building and went back to the ghetto.

There was no difference between the northwest side and the downtown area. She couldn't live in either place as a black person.

Even one church, opened by blacks on the northwest side of Grand Rapids in 1979 – 1980 was forced to close down because of threats by racists. They vandalised the church building and said they did not want any "niggers" on that side of town. They also called the church and told the minister and other church members they were going to shoot into the church and burn it down if they did not closed it down or if they showed up for church service just one more time. They said they were going to shoot the first person coming out of the church and go on shooting the rest still in the building.

They took the threats seriously and closed down the church and moved back to the ghetto.

Other blacks were attacked by white racists on the northwest side through the years; the few who tried to live there did not last long – they were forced to move out, mostly back to the ghetto.

One black family had their garage burned down. They were warned the entire house would be burned down if they did not move out of the house and the northwest side. They were told to go back to the ghetto.

A white woman who lived in a trailer park told the African American woman black people were not welcome even in trailer parks and she could not move in there. She went on to say white people in trailer parks did not like blacks, although it was a generalisation. But many of them, may be even the majority, may not want to live with blacks in trailer parks – or anywhere else.

The white woman was old enough to be the African woman's mother and was a friend of her mother. Even she admitted she had been prejudiced against blacks all her life but had now changed and accepted them. She also said it was hard to change and it took her a long time to do so.

She told the African American woman she even helped her landlords through the years to turn away prospective black tenants who wanted to rent apartments in the buildings where she lived or houses owned by her white landlords. She said she told blacks: "It has been rented," "It's not available," and so on.

She believed black people should live with their own kind in their own areas, the ghetto, where it was also safe for them unlike trailer parks or white areas where they could be attacked.

The African American woman also felt that she was safer in the ghetto than she was in white or predominantly white neighbourhoods. It is a sentiment shared by many blacks including those who support racial integration. People of all races have the right to free association. Free association is better than coercion and is more productive in pursuit of long-term integration.

Also, there is nothing wrong with living in the ghetto, whether you are black or white, if that is where you want to live or if black people just want to live with fellow blacks just like whites want to live with fellow whites – but without discriminating against or denying other people the right to live in those areas.

Black people in the ghetto don't even have a reputation of discriminating against whites and other nonblacks or telling them they can't live there and should go and live with fellow whites or with their own people in their own areas.

In the early 1980s, I knew one white man in Grand Rapids who worked near downtown and was old enough to be my father who told me it was safer for whites to go to the ghetto and even live there than it was for blacks to be in white areas. He used to go to the ghetto often and said he always felt safe there. I have heard stories similar to that a number of times.

The downtown area of Grand Rapids is so close to the ghetto, yet so far away in terms of perceptions of black people. Blacks do go downtown. Some of them even work there. But it is hostile territory for them in terms of residence, although there are some blacks who live there.

Even as late as 2020, there were places downtown where blacks were not welcome as tenants.

The owners of one major apartment building were sued in August 2019 for refusing to rent to blacks.

In June 2020, in another major apartment building, also downtown Grand Rapids, a black tenant was threatened and told to move out because the building was only for whites and "niggers" were not welcome. Racist messages including racial epithets were scrawled on his door: "No Blacks Allowed," "Move Nigger. We don't want you here," KKK," "WLM" (White Lives Matter).

A few years earlier, a young black woman, probably in her early twenties, moved to Grand Rapids from another city in Michigan (Battle Creek) and rented an apartment in one of the buildings in the downtown area. Not long after she moved in, she was greeted with racial epithets scrawled on her door. Her water was shut off; also her electricity. She appeared on local television and told how she was threatened ands terrorised in the building and forced to move out.

The other cases mentioned above were also covered by the local media; they were, and are, just a few among several.

The ghetto is the only place where blacks are supposed to live.

Collectively, ghettoes across America have through the years constituted a "homeland" for blacks, a part of what renowned black American sociologist, Professor E. Franklin Frazier, described as "a nation within a nation" although his description was about the "Negro church" in America which he said had the potential to have its own economy and become "a nation within a nation."

So does the ghetto where blacks spend hundreds of millions of dollars every year.

The black church itself is an embodiment of the ghetto in terms of demographics and sheer numbers. Millions of blacks in ghettoes across America are church members, thus constituting "a nation within a nation." They include blacks in Grand Rapids, a city which also, per capita, has a significant number of black churches as an integral part of the "black nation."

Marginalisaiton of blacks by the larger society is responsible for the creation of the "black nation." There would have been no need for one if integration were a practical reality.

The marginalisation of blacks has historical roots since slavery. But it also has been sanctioned by government policy through the years and even in contemporary times under the guise of a "colour-blind society," absolving the government, and the larger society, of any responsibility for the racial injustices against blacks whose plight and predicament is blamed on the victims themselves since the country, it is claimed, has done enough to correct racial injustices; hence the claim that the United States now is a colour-blind society in the legal sense – which it is – and in practice, which it is not.

Grand Rapids has been very much a part of this American experience which has shaped the destiny of black people in the city as much as it has the destiny of other blacks in other parts of the country, resulting in the creation of ethnic enclaves called ghettoes as the practical alternative to the motherland of black people – far removed from their ancestral homeland.

Racial segregation has played a very effective role in solidifying the existence and collective identity of these enclaves through the years.

What is sorely missing in an attempt to resolve this racial crisis is communication between blacks and whites as well as members of other races. It does take place, now and then, between individuals, groups – large and small – and in various institutions, but it is not sustained, and it is not long-term.

And it has to be meaningful in order to bring about fundamental change to achieve some kind of racial equality in relative terms, while acknowledging the harsh and painful reality that true racial equality will remain a Utopian ideal.

The conversation on race will become meaningful only when the majority of whites admit racism still exists not just as a problem but as a *major* problem and commit themselves, individually and collectively, to addressing it as a national crisis, not as an individual or local problem. But tackling it starts at the individual level, including soul-searching, admitting you are a racist if you are.

The ghetto, a product of segregation, also still exists. But it is no longer what it once was as "exclusively" black territory. Whites have, gradually through the years, been moving back into the inner cities, the "black homeland," buying houses and other property and raising rent. This has displaced blacks even in Grand Rapids and forced them to move out because they can't afford the high rent. That is what gentrification has meant to blacks across the nation.

Although gentrification has somewhat helped to integrate the inner city, an unintended outcome, it has at the same time strained race relations and has pushed blacks and whites apart by forcing blacks to move out of the ghetto as whites move in.

And in spite of the persistence of discrimination in housing and what I went through in Grand Rapids and what other blacks also experienced through the years, being denied housing, there were even back in the 1970s and 1980s black people living in different parts of the city except in some areas; and they still do today.

They have even penetrated some areas which were once forbidden territory. So, integration has succeeded, but in a limited way.

Discrimination against blacks, not just residential

segregation, *still is* a major problem in Grand Rapids. Employment is another area in which blacks are victimised. There is racial discrimination in other areas as is the case across the nation.

The incidents of raw-naked racism I have experienced, directly, through the years – as have many other blacks including those who were born and brought up in the United States – show that there are some whites who still don't want to accept blacks; it has nothing to do with my being foreign-born – it has to do with my blackness.

The racism I experienced did not surprise me at all as a black man in a predominantly white society where there are many racists. Many blacks have numerous incidents of racism to talk about including some in which black people have lost their lives.

So, it was nothing new to me; nothing shocking.

I had, after all, experienced racism in my home country, Tanganyika, as the country was known during British colonial rule and the early part of independence, an experience which hardened me towards racial insults and even had me accept racial segregation simply as a way of life that had to be accepted, tolerated or ignored, morally reprehensible as it is and because of its power dynamics. Segregation is not mutually acceptable but is imposed on those who are segregated by those who segregate; unlike mutually acceptable racial separation – where there is balance of power in terms of negotiation – but which is no less morally offensive because it equally rejects the brotherhood of man.

Yet, you don't have to integrate with people who don't want to integrate with you or whom you don't want to integrate with. You don't even have to associate with them. Free association is a fundamental right even if it means excluding people you don't like and don't want to associate with.

If you are black, you don't even have to associate with fellow blacks because they are black. And if you are white, you don't have to associate with fellow whites simply because they are white. Unfortunately, racists use the right to choose friends and to freely associate with the people you want to associate with – to defend and justify their racist beliefs when they oppose racial integration purely on racial grounds, not just because they only want to live with fellow whites.

I lived under segregation when I was growing up in Tanganyika. It was a form of apartheid reminiscent of South Africa under white minority rule.

We had separate facilities. Toilets were labelled "Africans," "Asians," and "Europeans." Some hotels were only for "Europeans" were labelled that way. Black people were not allowed to eat or drink there.

There were also separate schools for Europeans, Asians and Africans. Schools for Africans – black pupils and students – were the worst, poorly funded and with inadequate facilities.

The judicial system was biased against blacks; it was intended to serve whites and protect their privileged status. We had no recourse to law against whites.

When I was six years old, in primary school, I was bitten by a dog owned by a white couple. I was on my way to school. I was severely injured. The dog that bit me was large and could have easily killed me, little as I was. That was in 1956. I still have a highly visible scar on my right knee more than sixty years later.

Nothing was done, and nothing could be done against the white couple. It was colonial rule. We were just colonial subjects and did not have the same rights whites had.

The white couple, who lived about a quarter of a mile from my home, deliberately let their dogs (they had two) roam freely knowing full well they could attack us on our way to and from school everyday. We went by their house everyday which was near a public road. The road was not on their property. They still didn't care even though we walked on a public road. They also didn't care because they knew nothing could be done to them even if their dogs mauled us or killed us because were black children. Had we been white, they probably would,not have allowed their dogs to roam freely knowing they could attack and even kill us.

Even the primary school I attended had poor facilities because it was a school for black children. It was a government school and deliberately poorly funded by the British colonial government.

I therefore grew up under a system whose foundation was segregation, deliberately intended to keep members of different races separate and unequal.

I even remember the toilets we used, still labelled "Africans" even after independence in the sixties, and how nasty and filthy they were. I vividly remember one at the main bus station in the town of Mbeya, the capital of the Southern Highlands Province, where I came from.

That was the only public toilet black people could use. It was still labelled "Africans" years after independence, a chilling reminder of an inglorious past.

I remember using the toilet during holidays when I was a student, going to and from Songea Secondary School, a boarding school in southern Tanzania I attended from 1965 to 1968. I slept at the bus station, on the floor, with the other students as well as other passengers, all black. There were no chairs or benches. Whites and other nonwhites did not sleep there – if they had to, there would have been better facilities for them including chairs since colonial times.

There was also, in the town of Mbeya, the Mbeya Club and Mbeya Hotel exclusively for whites before independence; Mbeya School only for white children, mostly of British settlers; and a residential area for whites only, again mostly British.

I also spent a part of my childhood in Mbeya from 1954 to 1955. My family and I moved from Kigoma in the

Western Province to Morogoro in the Coast Province in 1952, and from Morogoro to Mbeya in 1954, a town in the Southern Highlands with a cool climate which reminded whites settlers of the temperate climate in Europe. It was also a town of racial contrasts, with whites enjoying privileged status in all areas of live sharply contrasted with the way we lived as black people.

Those are some of the striking parallels between life in Tanganyika during British colonial rule and life for blacks in the United States, especially in the South, during the era of segregation.

Therefore, racism is nothing new to me. And it is not an excuse for its victims not to try to do something with their lives, hard as it may be to achieve whatever they want to achieve because of the obstacles they face in pursuit of their goals.

So, there are problems. But let us also face this: In spite of the racial inequalities black people face in the United States, it remains a fact that they live in a country of abundant opportunities where it is possible for almost anybody to succeed in life.

The abundance of opportunities has blunted the sharp edges of racism even when it cuts deep into its victims. The successes of tens of millions of African Americans and black immigrants from Africa and the Caribbean in all areas of life is testimony to that.

But that is also where some blacks, born and brought up in the United States, clash with many black immigrants who contend that there are plenty of opportunities – jobs, education, skills training, self-employment and so forth – to succeed in the United States while some African Americans say racism is the biggest problem black people face in their lives. Both arguments have validity depending on individual circumstances.

Many blacks from Africa, and from the Caribbean, are very successful in the Untied States. Even when they admit racism exists, they don't see it as something that impedes progress. This is demonstrated by the large number of blacks born and brought up in the United States – African Americans – who have overcome racial barriers and become members of the middle class; it is millions of them. This shows that racism is not an insurmountable obstacle in all cases to succeed in life, although it is in many cases.

Also, there are many Black African immigrants and Afro-Caribbeans who simply ignore or overlook racism. They do that more than their brethren, black Americans do, who expect – and rightly so – to be treated equal to whites in terms of having opportunities to succeed life. The tolerance of racism, or their inability to feel it, has a lot to do with where they came from. They see a sharp contrast between the United States and their home countries in terms of opportunities available to succeed in life.

Their home countries have very few opportunities. That is why they left and came to "the land of milk and honey, "America the beautiful, from sea to shining sea." Even the sting of racism does not affect let alone discourage them from trying to succeed and forge ahead in life, sometimes – and quite often – reaching levels of success comparable to those of many white and black Americans, and even surpassing them.

It is not a level playing field – whites always have the upper hand – but it has not tipped scales against them in all areas of life.

One of the areas in which black African immigrants and others have achieved success is self-employment. They create opportunities for themselves. The American economy – as is the population – is so large and robust that even those who are self-employed, whether they are immigrants or American-born, find abundant opportunities to succeed in life.

Even writers who are immigrants or who live in the United States have the opportunity and the freedom to write what they want to write. They would not have been able to do that had they stayed in their home countries.

Highly educated immigrants who take any job including manual labour just to succeed in life are able to live on their income. They pay rent, buy food and meet other expenses even if their income is low. They would not have been to do that in their home countries. They would not have been able to earn enough to afford all that as they do in the United States.

So, America is a land of opportunity. But it also has its own problems just as other countries do.

Still, there is no question that the United States has a lot of opportunities for people to succeed in life. Otherwise foreigners, including African immigrants, would not be dying to come here, in spite of the racism that exists and which penetrates virtually every social fabric of the American society; a tapestry whose interwoven strands – so intricately done – reflect a truly rainbow nation and one of the first in the history of mankind to be so successful across the spectrum, demonstrated by its magnetic power drawing people from round the globe and round the clock.

People of all races should just acknowledge that racism will always exist.

There are many racists who are not even conscious of the fact that they are racist and think they treat blacks as equal human beings. They think some of the things they say about blacks are not racist but compliments. "He is very articulate," and so on.

Some of them may mean exactly that without any racial overtones or without implying "you are one of the few blacks" who speak that way. But many times, the implication is that if you are black, and you speak very well, you are different from other blacks, most of whom are not articulate, speak black English, and know nothing about grammar – that is why they speak broken English. But white people and many other nonblacks speak standard English.

That is why when United States Senator Harry Reid said Barack Obama did not speak with a "Negro dialect," he thought that was a compliment to him and other blacks who "speak proper," as they – black and white – like to say. As Reid himself stated in January 2008 when Obama was running for president, Obama was "light-skinned" and "with no Negro dialect, unless he wanted to have one."

The response he got, from blacks and even from some whites, was different. They interpreted his comment as a racist stereotype about blacks.

The same kind of stereotype about "exceptional" blacks was invoked by Joe Biden in February 2007 when he described Obama as "articulate" and "clean." Both men were running for president during that time. As Biden, who had a reputation for making jolting comments and raising eyebrows, stated:

"'I mean, you got the first mainstream African-American who is articulate and bright and clean and a nice-looking guy,' Biden said. 'I mean, that's a storybook, man.'" – ("Biden's Description of Obama Draws Scrutiny," CNN, 9 February 2007).

Black people are used to hearing that kind of language. "She is very clean," implying she is the exception because black people in general are "not clean," they are "shabby-looking" and with unkempt hair and so on.

It is the same thing when they use the term "nigger." They say they are just joking or using the term in the same way blacks use it when they call each other "nigger" as a term of endearment.

Some of them even say "we have our own niggers," as United States Senator Robert Byrd of West Virginia said, but somewhat differently, in an interview on race relations on 2 March 2001 broadcast nationwide:

"In an interview taped Friday (2 March) for 'Fox News Sunday,' Byrd, 83, was asked about race relations in the United States.

'They are much, much better than they've ever been in my lifetime,' Byrd said, but added that he believed people talk about race too much.

'My old mom told me, 'Robert, you can't go to heaven if you hate anybody.' We practice that. There are white niggers. I've seen a lot of white niggers in my time. I'm going to use that word. We just need to work together to make our country a better country, and I'd just as soon quit talking about it so much.'" – ("Top Senate Democrat Apologizes for Slur," *Inside Politics*, CNN, 4 March 2001).

He later apologized for using the term "niggers." He was once a member of the Ku Klux Klan.

Byrd was not only a member but a leader of the Ku Klux Klan (KKK) in his home state of West Virginia. He formed a KKK chapter in the early 1940s composed of 150 members he had recruited. They included his friends and associates. He was elected – without opposition – as the main leader, known as Exalted Cyclops in KKK language, of the local KKK unit.

He left the KKK decades ago. Yet, more than 50 years later, it was still easy for him to use the term "niggers" which he said "dates back to my boyhood" but "has no place in today's society."

The nonchalant yet disdainful and dismissive attitude towards blacks by some whites when using the term "nigger" may be shocking and even incomprehensible to some people of all races. But it is perfectly understandable in the broader context of race relations in America even today when looked at in terms of how society is structured as a racial hierarchy. Whites are top, blacks at the bottom.

There is no racial equality. And that reinforces racial stereotypes about black people even among white liberals who say they care about blacks. They also, like other whites, look at them through the lens of the larger society whose image of black people is distorted because it is refracted through the lens of racism, legitimising white superiority.

They cannot look at blacks any other way because the image of black people is shaped by the perceptions of the larger society of which they are an integral part as white people regardless of how, individually or collectively as liberals, they feel about blacks.

And many times, they don't mean what they say although they are the ones who are supposed to be friends of black people – liberals friends of "Negroes" – unlike other whites.

In a racially stratified society, in spite of the progress the country has made in terms of racial integration – and it has – even whites who may be shocked when they hear fellow whites call blacks "niggers," there is an implicit assumption on their part that black people are not really equal to whites. Society, the larger society which is white, says so. History says so; so does contemporary reality which demonstrates the utter futility of attempts to fully integrate society, and fully integrate blacks with whites and even with members of other races who also don't accept black people as equals.

The black American experience is inextricably linked with the dominance of the white race in the American society and is a product of such domination, prompting James Baldwin once to say he was born a man to suffer and a nigger to be despised.

What is consoling is that for every racist, there is at least one person who is not. And therein lies hope for redemption.

Even some of the most racist people have the capacity to conquer evil and accept people of other races as their brothers and sisters. As Dr. Martin Luther King said in a speech in St. Louis, Missouri, on 22 March 1964:

"We must learn to live together as brothers or perish together as fools."

If some whites say what they say about black people because they don't know them – they can't if they don't want to interact or work with them on matters of mutual concern – one wonders if they really know themselves as much as they think they do in a society whose reality in terms of race relations is distorted by prejudice and whose destiny is collectively determined by the destinies of all of its people – black, white, brown – with whites being dominant. As James Baldwin stated:

"Whatever white people do not know about Negroes reveals, precisely and inexorably, what they do not know about themselves." – (James Baldwin, "Letter from a Region in My Mind," 9 November 1962, in *The New Yorker,* 17 November 1962).

They all live in a society where they cannot entirely avoid each other. Therefore they will have to accept each other as a people who are bound by fate and who share a common destiny regardless of how they feel.

There is no America as a society without either of them. Both have created this society, have shaped its destiny, and will continue to share it as long as they live. Black people are as American as white people are. They don't need to be accepted by whites to be American. Only their right as Americans has to be accepted.

Black people don't seek acceptance on terms stipulated by whites – that is capitulation to white might. They seek acceptance on the basis of mutually acceptable terms to achieve racial equality. Many blacks don't care if white people don't like them or if they don't accept them as equals or as friends as long as they don't interfere with their rights as equal citizens. And they can work together for mutual benefit without necessarily being friends or relatives-in-law.

James Baldwin put this subject of delicate relations between blacks and whites in its proper perspective and context when he stated the following in his essay, "Letter From a Region in My Mind." in *The Fire Next Time*:

"I do not know many Negroes who are eager to be 'accepted' by white people, still less to be loved by them; they, the blacks, simply don't wish to be beaten over the head by the whites every instant of our brief passage on this planet. White people in this country will have quite enough to do in learning how to accept and love themselves and each other, and when they have achieved this—which will not be tomorrow and may very well be never—the Negro problem will no longer exist, for it will no longer be needed."

My American experience has broadened and deepened my understanding of race relations between blacks and whites after living in a society that is predominantly white and in which blacks are on the periphery of the mainstream in terms of power dynamics over which they have no control because of their powerlessness and minority status.

It is this minority status and powerlessness which makes them vulnerable to the whims and caprice of even some of the weakest members of the white community but who consider themselves to be powerful because they are members of the larger society and identify with those who are in power because they fellow whites.

It is also the larger society, white society, which defines Black America and teaches foreigners about black Americans: what kind of people they are. Africans born and brought up in Africa are among those foreigners. And a part of the larger society which teaches that is the media.

When foreigners, especially black, come to the United

States and learn the truth about black Americans, especially when they live with them in the black community, mainly the ghetto, they find out they have been taught lies.

Those lies are a product of racism intended to portray black people as irresponsible members of society who don't even want to do anything to help themselves – except commit crime and live on welfare – and have to wait for whites to help them. It is myth that is propagated and amplified by racists to justify their claim that blacks don't deserve equal rights and don't even deserve to be American and to be an integral part of society.

But they *are* American, they are an integral part of the American society, and they are going nowhere. As Martin Luther King said in one of his recorded speeches:

"We ain't going *nowhere*."

The attitude of some whites when they hurl insults at black people, including racial epithets, shows that they don't accept them as fellow Americans and as equal human beings who are entitled to the same rights they are.

Black people are human beings like other human beings. They are also individuals just like other human beings.

The tendency to generalise when white people talk and write about blacks has to do with racism. "All blacks, at least most of them, commit crime or are involved in some kind of illegal activity, unlike whites. They're dangerous."

At the other end of the spectrum, from the perspective of some blacks: "All whites, at least most of them, are racist."

It is perceptions and misconceptions like these which perpetuate the race problem in America, a problem some whites use to justify control over blacks because they are "out of control" and need to be "controlled," thus perpetuating white domination.

If the race problem is resolved, there will be no such domination, a terrifying prospect for racists. Racial equality will end the race problem.

So, keep the race problem going to justify white domination of blacks – in a country founded on liberty and equality, twin pillars of the republic!

Not only will the race problem continue to exist – racism will become even more potent and sometimes ruthlessly public as it did in the Trump era. That was when the country had a president who mobilised white voters during his presidential campaign launched from a racist platform saying, "'We are going to make America great again." It was coded language. He meant "make America white again" after the country had its first black president, Barack Obama.

Had Obama not been elected president, there would have been no Trump as president of the United States.

Trump's victory was a result of a white backlash against blacks. Millions of whites were angry a black man won and occupied the White House for eight years. It was time to hit back and elect a white man to "cleanse" the White House in a retaliatory response that led to the election of a president who was clearly a racist and lacked racial sensitivity and even called black African countries "shithole countries."

It is true millions of whites voted for Obama. But the majority of the white voters did not vote for him. It was a coalition of voters across racial lines, forming a rainbow coalition, who got Obama elected as president.

Some of Trump's supporters who regretted voting for him should also acknowledge that if they did so in retaliation against Obama's victory, they got what they wanted. Trump's victory was the reward they got from the racism they harboured against Obama and they should be proud of it because that is what they wanted.

There were, of course, those who voted for Trump as a vote against Hillary Clinton. They did not like her. And there were those who were not ready for another eight years of a Clinton in the White House after Hilary's husband, Bill Clinton, served for two terms as president. There were also those who voted for Trump because he was a Washington outsider and believed him when he said he was going to "drain the swamp."

What is sometimes ignored is the major role racism played in helping Trump win and the damage it did to country's image abroad where he was widely denounced as a racist.

It was not the first time white Americans elected a racist as president. There have other American presidents in the past who were also racist even in modern times – Eisenhower, Nixon, Reagan. But it was the first time in modern times that they elected someone who was openly racist and who was proud of his credentials as a racist and white nationalist.

Never did I imagine that the United States would one day have a president who would act like a tin pot dictator of a Third World country with all delusions of grandeur; nor did I ever think that a great nation like the United States would one day have a leader who could have some of the same characteristics as the brutal and flamboyant Ugandan dictator Idi Amin who even called himself "King of Scotland," "Conqueror of the British Empire," and "Ruler of the Universe."

That is what racism did to the United States when white voters decided to elect a racist as president. And America reaped bitter fruits for betraying its sacred principles, tarnishing the image of one of the greatest nations in the history of mankind.

That is the price you pay for being racist. You elect a racist president and he ends up being an embarrassment to the nation and the laughing stock of the world reminiscent of Idi Amin who made history and earned the unenviable distinction of being a buffoon of incomparable stature in the 1970s; both populist leaders, also both with delusions of grandeur, Amin also having gained international notoriety for killing more than 300,000 people and expelling the entire Asian community from Uganda including those who were citizens. Trump also excelled in his own way as an international pariah.

Since the last president, before Trump, tried to take the country back to the "dark ages" of racial equality, it was time to make America white again by electing a white man to occupy the White House which had been tarnished by the first black president.

Voters knew they were voting for a racist. Trump did not hide his feelings about that. He wanted the whole world to know what type of person he was.

During the presidential campaign, he used racist language to mobilise white voters. He invoked white identity as a rallying cry for his supporters, whipping up racist sentiments against blacks and other nonwhites whom they felt were not good enough to be Americans and don't belong here. His incendiary rhetoric reverberated beyond American borders and round the globe.

Appalled by Trump's bilious rage and vitriol against blacks, Nigerian professor and Nobel laureate, Wole Soyinka, who was teaching in the United States during that time stated in a television interview:

"The rhetoric that got him there was rhetoric against the black people....

Did you follow the campaign? As far as I was concerned, that man should have been arrested and tried a long time ago for hate speeches. It's as elementary as that.

I couldn't believe what I was hearing. What was worse, I couldn't believe the sight of hordes of ecstatic supporters. Every outrageous statement, every racist statement, every xenophobic statement was applauded by wildly cheering hordes. And I said, well, this society is changing backwards right before our very eyes.

The United States had moved, had progressed so far

that we on the African continent could boast that we now had a contemporary descendant of the African continent ruling the United States. And suddenly, somebody is making speeches which are supposed to reverse those gains, and had masses of people cheering. And this at a particular period, where as I said, in one of those interviews, by the way, when I said I was getting out, I said, did this man not realise that he was giving yardage to the phenomenon of black killings in the United States? I said in that interview that it was as if the police had evolved a new fraternity requirement for remaining members of the police force and that was to go out and kill a black man.

You saw the rise, the protests across the country, one killing one day replicated over there, and during that period, somebody wants to be the leader of a nation, is giving xenophobic speeches.

The damage is already done whether we like it or not. People's minds, extreme right-wing, has been empowered across the nation. The notion, this sense of undeclared impunity, especially against minorities, has been encouraged, and I would see it enhanced; whether he even wants to do a 180-degree turn, the fact is that hatred has been sown, the country has been further divided." – (Wole Soyinka, "I Will Destroy My American Green Card If Trump Wins," October 28, 2016; "Donald Trump's Election: Soyinka Explains Decision on Green Card," December 5, 2016; "Wole Soyinka Renounces US Green Card," December 1, 2016).

When Trump won, his supporters were thrilled. White supremacists cheered. They said he campaigned for the same things they had been advocating all along. He embodied their ideals and aspirations. As white supremacist Jared Taylor – the intellectual godfather of white nationalism in contemporary America – who campaigned for Trump and lived and worked in West

Africa for quite some time, said in one of his speeches, "Whites Hand Trump a Great Victory":

"This is one of the great fights to the finish in American political history....

Donald Trump won because ordinary Americans, overwhelmingly white Americans, proved they are not the obedient zombies our rulers wish we were.

This was a vote for America as a distinct nation with a distinct people who deserve a government devoted to that people.

Donald Trump, a billionaire, was a man who said what ordinary Americans feel. People voted for Donald Trump for a lot of reasons. They are sick of professional politicians. They resent media elites who treat them like fools....

Millions of whites voted for Donald Trump because of a dawning sense of the importance of race. They took notice when he pointed out that some of the Mexicans sneaking into the country are criminals. They were thrilled when he talked about building a wall. And they were delighted when he said he would send home illegals, keep out Muslims, and end birthright citizenship.

Donald Trump never said that part of America's basic identity is whiteness. But he has made it very clear that certain people don't belong here. And that is what our rulers hate most about him because they think everyone belongs here. That is what Hillary believes....Those of us who believe Americans are a distinct people have to be rejected. Well, Hillary, you got rejected.

Actual Americans reject the idea that America is whoever manages to sneak in. They reject the idea that America become Hispanic or Asian or Muslim or Hindu or anything at all and still be American. They reject the idea that the founding stock of this country can be switched out and replaced with anyone from anywhere....

It is true that he won 67 percent of whites who don't

have a college education. But they haven't been brainwashed by lefty college professors and, this is even more important, they are the people who actually have to live with the diversity that Hillary claims to love.

What's more, Mr. Trump actually won more college educated white voters than Hillary did, 49 to 45 (percent), with the rest voting for minor candidates.

The fact is, this is the first presidential election in which white people began to vote like everyone else; in other words, in their own interests.

Our rulers take it for granted that blacks and Hispanics and Asians and everyone else have interests that they can push forward as hard as they can. After decades of encouraging nonwhites to do that, our rulers are shocked, *shocked*, to discover that white people have discovered they have interests too. That is Donald Trump's great achievement: to have been the standard bearer, even if unconsciously, of white interests.

The sleeping giant has been stirring for some time, and Mr. Trump gave it a voice and a reason to act. And what white people have done is to elect a man who has been called literally every name in the book....

By electing Donald Trump, the voters smashed countless taboos. When Donald Trump talks about Mexican criminals, when he says our system of anchor-babies citizens is crazy, when he says we need to take a hard look at Muslims, he now says these things as the future president of the United States. He cannot be ignored. This means we are in a new era. Americans will speak a new language.

This is also a new era for the Republican party. It better be anyway....Donald Trump proved that voters cared about the nation and its people. Republicans had better learn. He did a huge favor to the so-called conservative intellectuals too. If they are going to be relevant, they are going to have to build an intellectual framework for what voters care about. And that framework must include a recognition of the importance and significance of race.

Here is an idea Republicans and conservatives can start with. Whites are a minority in 370 counties in the United States. What percentage of these counties did Hillary win? 84 percent. Donald Trump won just 16 percent. Chew on that idea for a while.

And finally, I have a word about the people who said they would leave the country if Mr. Trump won. That includes Barbra Streisand, John Stewart, Cher, Miley Cyrus, Whoopi Goldberg, Lena Dunham, Spike Lee, Al Sharpton, and plenty of others. Oh, fellows, it is time to clear out. Supreme Court Justice Ruth Bader Ginsbsurg said she would move to New Zealand if Donald Trump became president. Ruth baby, *astalavista*." – (Jared Taylor, "Whites Hand Trump a Great Victory," Youtube, published on November 9, 2016; Jared Taylor, quoted in Michael J. Robinson, *Why Democrats Lost the Presidential Election and How they Can Win Next Time,* Scotts Valley, California, USA: Kindle Publishing, 2017, pp. 57 – 59).

Before Trump was Obama, the first black president. Yet the country was not ready for a black president. The white backlash which propelled Trump to the White House is proof of that.

Obama came before his time and too early to help bring about fundamental change in race relations. After his eight-year presidency ended, race relations were no better than they were before he became president, demonstrated by Trump's rise to power in a retaliatory move by white voters against his victory.

Had it not been for a broad and sophisticated coalition of non-white voters and some whites – a minority – who were genuinely committed to improving race relations and bringing about fundamental change in the American society, Obama would not have won and become the nation's first black president. He did, of course, and that was the end of Black Moses, as some of his supporters rechristened him, in terms of being an agent for transforming America into a society of genuine racial equality.

Obama's victory did not come from a majority of white voters but from a coalition of forces of nonwhites and many whites who supported him. In terms of numbers, fewer whites voted for him than those who didn't because of racism. The majority of whites did *not* vote for him.

Without a very high voter turnout among blacks, Hispanics, other nonwhites and whites who supported him in a very sophisticated coalition of voters, he would *not* have won the election.

Yet even a significant number of whites who were prejudiced against blacks voted for Obama, not because they withheld their racial prejudice against him; they voted for him because he was a fellow Democrat, hence a vote against the Republican candidate more than it was for Obama. They were voting for their party.

Then came Trump who was openly supported by white racists. They included racist intellectuals such as Jared Taylor who, for years, has tried to win acceptance of white nationalism in the mainstream by being polished and refined in his arguments without using crude language typical of rabid white supremacists.

Taylor was right in his assessment of the country's political climate and Trump's chances of winning the presidency by mobilisng white voters – he did not need black and Hispanic voters to win. And he won.

Other whites, besides white supremacists, also voted for Trump because he identified with them in terms of their interests as whites even if they were not racist like Taylor and other advocates of whites supremacy.

To win the presidency, Trump focused on whites voters – almost to the exclusion of black and Hispanic as well as other non-white voters – and in counties that were overwhelmingly white which would tip scales in his favour and enable him to win electoral votes, hence the presidency, in highly contested states.

The strategy worked. As Jared Taylor stated, Trump should focus on mobilising white voters who constitute 65 percent of the electorate to win the presidency. He was right. As Jared Taylor put it:

"Millions of whites voted for Donald Trump because of a dawning sense of the importance of race....Donald Trump's great achievement (is) to have been the standard bearer, even if unconsciously, of white interests." – (Ibid., p. 80).

After Trump won, Taylor celebrated. "I was thrilled," he said.

I have witnessed the significance of race – and its negative impact – in my life growing up in colonial Tanganyika and even after independence when my home country was still known as Tanganyika, and even later when it became Tanzania after uniting with Zanzibar to form one nation. I have also witnessed the significance of race – and its devastating effects – after living in the United States for many years.

One of the most tragic consequences of racism in the United States is police brutality against blacks more than anybody else. Even many whites concede that, demonstrated by their involvement in protests against racism when George Floyd was brutally choked to death by a white police officer in Minneapolis, Minnesota, in May 2020.

The protests, which went on nationwide everyday for more than two months, and in many other countries, signalled the beginning of what seemed to be the second civil rights movement in an era when racism had become more covert than overt yet often reared its ugly head in its most brutal form against blacks.

The protests, and even the riots during those protests,

were clearly a referendum on American leadership on how it addresses the fundamental problem of racial injustices against its black citizens, thus questioning its commitment to the core principles of liberty and equality for all upon which this nation was founded. It is a challenge that goes to the very soul of the nation.

The savage and racist murder of George Floyd exposed and highlighted the hypocrisy and contradictions inherent in the system which deliberately discriminates against blacks while its leaders profess equality for all.

Another brutal act by white police officers which also galvanised opposition to abuse of power by the police and also got international attention was the vicious attack on Rodney King, a black man, on 3 March 1991. He was savagely beaten by four white police officers. Yet they were acquitted of all charges. Their acquittal triggered riots in Los Angeles, California, from 29 April to 4 May in 1992.. They were some of the worst riots in American history. The uprising was also the costliest and deadliest in the nation's history up to that time.

There have been many Rodney Kings since then. And there were many Rodney Kings before there was Rodney King.

In many cases, just being black is enough to cost black people their lives.

Just stepping out of your house becomes a matter of serious concern for a black person, a matter of life and death, fearing you may not return home alive if you have an encounter with the police even if you have done nothing wrong.

It is usually white police officers who pose the greatest danger to blacks. But others do as well, including Hispanic and Asian police officers who are equally hostile to blacks or don't care about their well-being. Philando Castile, a black man, was brutally murdered by a Hispanic police officer, Jeronimo Yanez, another case that got nationwide and international attention.

He shot at him seven times, and hit him five times, only a few feet away – less than 10 feet – when Castile was sitting in the car with his girlfriend and his girlfriend's daughter who was in the backseat in spite of the fact that he complied with everything the police officer asked him to do; the whole incident videotaped, showing Castile did nothing wrong and posed no threat to the police officer. Castile was driving the car.

Yet, as in many other brutal killings of black people by white and other non-black police officers, Yanez was also acquitted of all charges.

Even one of my nieces, a teenager, asked me what was going on and why they were killing black people like that. She wrote me from Tanzania and was horrified by the murders, as many other people were in different parts of Africa and elsewhere around the world, and said I should write a book about that. It was after George Floyd was choked to death. She said the title of my book should be *I Can't Breathe*.

White people don't have to worry about losing their lives at the hands of the police just because they are white, or worry about being denied opportunities in life, the way black people are, simply because they are white. White people have the luxury to do anything they want to do in life – almost anywhere in the world. It is black people who are outcasts, and at the bottom of the barrel, even in their own countries in Africa and elsewhere.

Black lives mean nothing, absolutely nothing, to many whites and other nonblacks.

It is and always has been that way throughout American history since slavery, an inglorious past notorious for lynchings of black people through the years including cropping – chopping off feet of slaves who tried to run away – in a nation supposedly founded on the twin ideals of liberty and equality, twin pillars of the Republic, underscored by the invocation, "In God We Trust," that has been – or is supposed to be – an integral part of the

American character and identity as a nation.

The majority of blacks are deeply suspicious of the police and other law enforcement officers. Their suspicion extends to the larger society. Many of them believe they are not fully accepted as equal members of the American society for one simple reason – because they are black and for no other reason than that.

This has led to a feeling of insecurity across black America, with blacks fearing for their lives whenever they have an encounter with the police. Whites don't have that kind of fear. Insecurity, any kind of insecurity, creates unstable societies which can explode anytime.

Almost every black community across the nation, including Grand Rapids, is a potential tinderbox. And it all can be traced to racism, a malady afflicting the larger society, not just law enforcement agencies which, in spite of their reputation for being racist or racially insensitive, have many officers who try their best to be fair to everybody regardless of race; some of them don't, and deliberately so.

Yet they are all a part of a system that serves the ruling class and other powerful interests in society, almost all predominantly white constituting the white power structure, at the expense of the poor of *all* races although poor whites are treated better than blacks and other minorities but are still victims of those in power; also at the expense of *all* blacks and other racial minorities regardless of their economic status.

That is why even some black law enforcement officers are no better than their white counterparts in their treatment of their fellow blacks – they all serve the same powerful interests in society, with black people being the most disadvantaged in terms of justice.

The major problem is the larger society, the incubator of racism which finds comfortable accommodation in the hearts and minds of racists who include many whites who may be sympathetic to the plight of black people as victims of racism yet think they are better than blacks morally, intellectually and in any other conceivable way except in sports, singing and dancing.

Law enforcement agencies are an integral part of the larger society. They embody and reflect the values and attitudes, virtues and vices – including racial views and beliefs as well as insensitivities – of the larger society which is predominantly white and whose moral vision of a better America for all is constantly challenged and contradicted by the racial injustices it perpetrates against its black members and other racial minorities.

The country has made some progress in terms of race relations. Yet there is one question America has faced since its founding and which goes to the very heart and soul of the nation. It still haunts the nation and it is an existential question. It is also a moral question. It has to do with the presence of black people in America and what to do with them. It is an issue – unresolved, irritating and perplexing – that has put the greatest country on earth and in the history of mankind in a moral quandary.

Black people are in America, and have been in America, since its founding. They laid the foundation of the country as slaves and they continued to build it throughout its history.

The dilemma the country faces, accept them or reject them, is not just a moral choice – it jeopardises the very existence of the nation as a stable entity.

Black people cannot be wished away – they are not going to disappear. And they cannot be ignored in a country whose very existence is not even predicated on the premise of racial purity, yet acts as if it were, demonstrated by its non-acceptance of blacks as equal and full citizens in the fullest sense of the term, in practice, not just in terms of theoretical or limited acceptance.

The questions white people should ask themselves concerning their treatment of black people are these:

"Why are we doing this to them? What have they done to us to deserve such treatment? Why don't we want to accept them? Why do we accept some people, such as Asians, but not black people who have been with us longer, much longer – since the founding of the nation – than other people have? In fact, they are among the first Americans, the most American of all Americans besides Native Americans in terms of how long they have been here. The first African slaves arrived in Virginia in August 1619, long before most of our European ancestors did. Yet we say we are more American than they are. Why?"

Native Americans even lost their land, and countless lives, when they were invaded and conquered by Europeans and their descendants – white Americans. And they still feel the pain, an enduring legacy of the racial injustices they suffered and continue to suffer long after they were conquered.

I remember one incident involving a white man and a Native American which reminded me of that.

In April 1974, I went to Norman, Oklahoma. I wanted to attend the University of Oklahoma. I was still a student in Detroit but wanted to transfer to another school where there was a possibility of getting a full scholarship.

I travelled from Detroit to Oklahoma City on a Greyhound bus. When I arrived in Oklahoma City, I had to transfer to another bus, Lonestar, to get to Norman, as the bus went on its way to Texas. Norman is about 20 miles south of Oklahoma City.

As I was waiting for the Lonestar bus at the Greyhound bus station, I saw a Native American man, who was probably in his late sixties or seventies, drinking some water from a water fountain at the station. I remember he was tall, at least six feet and two to three inches.

After he drank some water for about half a minute, he seemed to be getting ready to leave. But when he turned around, he saw a white man who had been standing right behind him, also waiting to drink some water. Instead of leaving, the Native American turned back to the water fountain and started drinking some water again. He kept on drinking, probably for at least two minutes. He turned to look at the white man again who was still standing behind him, and again started drinking some water for another minute or so. He looked at the white man again and left, walking away slowly.

Other people at the bus station, almost all white, also noticed that. They were looking at both of them.

It was clear the Native American was not that thirsty. He seemed to be punishing the white man for the evils and injustices whites had done to his people. It was one man's protest, probably repeated by others in different ways, including blacks, whose impact may be minimal in correcting racial injustices but cathartic on an individual level even if it is only for temporary relief.

Black people being no strangers to racial injustices can easily understand why that Native American did what he did. They have been victims of racial injustices more than anybody else except Native Americans.

And they have engaged in protests, collectively and individually, probably more than Native Americans have, but only because of their superiority in numbers not because they have a more resilient spirit than the indigenous people do.

Black people are also the most visible symbol of racial hatred and, in many cases, the most victimised.

It is a moral issue. But it is also a moral challenge demanding initiatives by whites, complemented by efforts and the involvement of black people, to solve the problem. And it is a problem of ages.

Different people think they are so different that they cannot live together in harmony; it is a myth because they can and they have in different parts of the world throughout man's history.

The refusal by many whites to acknowledge this

reality, simple yet profound, perpetuates the problem inexorably leading them to seek what they may think is a simple solution to a complex problem: simply ignore blacks and that will be the end of the race problem in America. Just ignore them.

But ignoring black people is not enough. It is not only not enough – it has been tried and it has failed. It has failed to solve the race problem, if that is even a solution at all.

The needle of the moral compass points only in one direction, of reconciliation and accommodation of the races, even if it is sometimes deflected to point towards perpetual conflict and annihilation, which is not a choice at all.

The moral ambivalence of many whites who equivocate on urgent matters of racial justice – critical to the very survival of the nation – is symptomatic of a bigger problem the nation has faced since its founding. And that is its unwillingness to accept black people as full human beings equal to whites and bound by their common humanity. That is still the moral issue confronting America and one that it has to contend with in the twentieth-first century; not just for a few years, or even for a few decades, but throughout the century.

When people like Jared Taylor – there are many others of his ilk – say Trump won the presidential election because he knew the importance of race by appealing to white voters – he virtually ignored the rest yet won because of white voters – he challenges the assumptions of common bonds of humanity which unite people of all races, including blacks whom he despises so much yet who are a part of him as much as he is a part of them for simply being equally human, regardless of what he thinks or believes to be the genetic "inferiority" of black people because of their "low" mental capacity.

You cannot diminish the humanity of others without diminishing yours. Regardless of how different we may look, we are mirror images of each other as fellow human beings whose intrinsic worth is not embodied in physical features.

There is no black blood just as there is no white blood. There is human blood, one blood. And we share blood across the colour line. That shows how "different" we are, to the consternation of racists.

Many white racists in hospitals across the nation have their lives saved everyday during blood transfusions when they get blood from black people, donated by black people. Blacks who have donated the blood have the same blood type white patients have. The blood type of the white patients is different from the blood type of their fellow whites who are even their brothers and sisters by blood and race. Yet they have the same blood type some blacks have, the same people they hate so much.

There is another dimension to that. Given the history of the country, many whites, tens of millions of them including white supremacists and other racists, have African blood and ancestry they revile and detest so much. Yet they could not have been born without it. Even if they have just one drop of African blood, they could *not* have been born without it.

There are many whites who know they are not just white but don't want their children or anybody else to know that. They include white supremacists.

Professor Mark D. Shriver, a genetics specialist at Pennsylvania State University, says 30 per cent of white Americans have African ancestors, including himself. He says he has 22 per cent West African ancestry. Yet he looks just white. He said his mother knew about their African ancestry but kept it secret.

Whites constitute at least 70 percent of the American population. With 30 percent of them having African ancestry – that is tens of millions of them!

Those are the kind of indissoluble bonds, natural ties, which exist between members of different races in the

United States. They also bind them together as members of one nation and determine the fate of the nation whose existence is predicated on the acceptance of equality for all.

The history, the blood, the ideals and values of one indivisible nation under God, such are the bonds that bind Americans together as members of a nation forged on the anvil of diversity which has become *the* microcosm of mankind.

Every race, tribe, creed, ethnic group, country and region round the globe is represented in the United States as an integral part of it. There is no other country on earth that is so diverse in its demographic composition, yet so united. Yet the dominant group, in a predominantly white country, puts a premium on race and, in fact, exactly for that reason. It is mostly white, therefore it is a white nation, the argument goes.

Tragically, the importance of race in man's history has been at the expense of others and to the detriment of other people's well-being. That is the trajectory man has taken since the beginning and it is bound to take him towards self-destruction, a destiny even some of the most hardened racists may not want to face.

I have seen what race glorification has done to people in Africa, including my home country when it was colonial Tanganyika and even after independence and when the former island nation of Zanzibar was almost engulfed in a racial conflagration – black African versus Arab. I have also witnessed its corrosive effect on relations between blacks and whites in the years I have lived in the United States. And I shudder at the consequences.

The United States is not a collision course between the races. But if it compromises its vision of a just society, it undermines its sacred principles of liberty and equality, twin pillars of the republic, upon which it was conceived even though in practical terms it was founded on slavery – outright enslavement of millions of Africans – with consequences too ghastly to contemplate.

Trump during his presidency became the embodiment of this nightmare.

When a country has such leaders, fanning ambers of racial hatred, prospects for racial reconciliation become bleak.

The country has had such leaders before. That it can have them again in this era of so-called "post-racial" America is a terrifying prospect. And as before, throughout the nation's history, blacks will again, and again, be at the centre of this maelstrom swirling around them.

The moral foundations of the nation are undermined when its leaders who are supposed to uphold standards of moral excellence and act as the conscience of the nation express views that are antithetical to the principles on which this nation was founded; views which are embraced by those who think this country belongs to them alone to the total exclusion of others who don't look like them.

They are toxic views. And they are lethal. Yet they easily seep into the mainstream of society and gain legitimacy because they are a product of the collective conscience of the nation: the leaders.

Such leaders have an impaired moral vision, if they have any at all, and do not have the moral authority to be leaders. Yet, they win elections, and rise to power even without elections in some countries, by inspiring fear of the enemy within – blacks and other nonwhites including nonwhite immigrants in the American context – and by invoking patriotism in a perverted way ostensibly to preserve, protect and promote the interests of the nation as a whole. Morality means nothing to them, as has been demonstrated in a crude way in the era of Trump.

The country witnessed a great increase in the number of white supremacist groups under his leadership and a resurgence of white nationalism as never before but drew little condemnation from the larger society because white nationalism became an accepted ideology among many whites, legitimsied by Trump's racist rhetoric expressed in coded language. Yet his message was clear and continued to inspire and embolden many racists to the detriment of the well-being of minorities and even the nation itself as a whole.

Yet, there are many people, of *all* races, who find those views to be reprehensible and morally repugnant. And they reject them vehemently and try to sway the nation in the right direction with moral suasion. Unfortunately, in a world bereft of conscience, moral suasion is not persuasive enough; which explains, although only partly, the emergence of people like Trump on the national scene and the ease with which they have been able to dominate the political landscape with far-reaching consequences for the nation. And they have found acceptance and comfortable accommodation in an ideological camp whose members are known for their hostility towards blacks. It is the ideological camp of conservatism.

But, in fairness, black people must also accept responsibility for their own actions over which they have control, not for problems – structural and institutional – they face as a result of historical and contemporary injustices perpetrated against them by the larger society; a society that has rejected them.

What, for example, explains the exclusion of blacks from the suburbs where they collectively constitute only a very small percentage nationwide?

Crime, a highly volatile issue with racial connotations blaming *all* blacks for committing *all* that crime, is given as one reason – if not as the main reason – for keeping them out of there; so is the stereotype, "all blacks look alike," and therefore can't tell the difference between a black robber and a black law-abiding citizen in the suburbs and everywhere else.

Yet, the people who are rejected and excluded from getting homes in suburban areas are not the "riffraff" from the ghetto; they are respectable members of society including highly successful blacks in all professions comparable to their white counterparts.

Many whites always – *always* – try to find excuses to justify their acts of racial injustices against blacks, Compounding the felony – and it *is* a felony – is the accusation that black people are fully responsible for their condition, any condition they are in, and for *all* the problems they face as if there is no racism which is responsible for that, thus absolving the larger society, white society, of any responsibility.

The truth lies somewhere in between.

Yet moral suasion, although not effective in many cases, is better than the alternative, conflict, and may be the only viable option – and the last hope for mankind as it has been since the beginning – in a world locked in perpetual conflict with the forces of evil.

There are people of conscience. But they don't do enough to help bring about fundamental change whose success may even change some people who don't care about morality. Even some racists, to whom morality means nothing, may change their attitude towards blacks, as indeed they have throughout the nation's history, although they are few; a sharp contrast with those who are locked in a vicious cycle of hate – feeding on itself – and don't even make an attempt to break out of it because they are comfortable living in their own world where they reject the humanity of others without realising that, by doing so, they also deny the basis of their own humanity which is universal and includes the humanity of black people.

Yet another harsh reality people have to face is that forced integration never works; in the short term, yes; in the long run, no. It only infuriates its opponents. That partly, if not largely, explains why millions of whites have fled to the suburbs – white flight – running away from blacks and why many schools in large cities across the nation are still predominantly black years after busing, especially in the seventies.

You cannot force people to accept you just as you cannot force them to love you.

True racial integration comes from the heart out of genuine commitment to racial equality and to the brotherhood of man. It is genuine acceptance of fellow human beings as your brothers and sisters. If you don't accept them, you cannot integrate with them even if you are forced to live with them. Such integration is hollow.

I witnessed stiff resistance to busing in Boston, Massachusetts, in 1975 when I was a student at Wayne State University in Detroit. Buses full of students, I among them, left our campus for Boston to oppose violence and support school integration. We also attended a mass rally where Roy Wilkins, head of the NAACP, spoke in support of school busing and racial integration in general.

People came from all over the country in convoys of buses after violence in the streets by white opponents of busing made headlines across the nation and put the city in the spotlight, highlighting the racial hatred that had gripped Boston in spite of its reputation as one of the most liberal and racially tolerant cities in the United States.

Busing still failed to genuinely integrate schools, not just in Boston, but across the country.

All that demonstrates one simple truth in the American context.

Black people have not yet been fully accepted as equal citizens in all areas of life in spite of the progress the country has made in race relations especially since the civil rights movement which reached its peak in the late sixties.

Decades later, it is the same pattern, the same experience, and the same humiliation and racial injustices, only in varying degrees. And it happens everyday in different parts of the country. As James Baldwin stated:

"Negroes want to be treated like men: a perfectly straightforward statement containing seven words. People who have mastered Kant, Hegel, Shakespeare, Marx, Freud and the Bible find this statement utterly impenetrable." – (James Baldwin, "Fifth Avenue, Uptown," *Esquire,* July 1960; and in James Baldwin, *Nobody Knows My Name*, New York: Dial Press, 1961).

Almost forty years later, Professor Nathan Glazer, a highly distinguished scholar in his field and author of *Beyond the Melting Pot* which was partly written by Professor Daniel Patrick Moynihan, expressed similar sentiments when he stated in his book which was published in 1997, *We Are All Multiculturalists Now*, that the fundamental problem "is the refusal of other American to accept blacks."

Yet all the racial insults – including "African monkey" or "African monkeys" which are hurled at us even by other nonblacks not just by whites – as well as injustices black people are subjected to have never dampened my spirits; nor have they dampened the spirits of millions of other blacks. In fact, racism can be an incentive to succeed in life – victims try harder at whatever they do or try to achieve in life.

Besides a resilient spirit, one of the biggest weapons in my arsenal against racism is experience.

I have experienced racism since childhood and even almost got killed because of that when, as a six-year-old, I was viciously attacked by a dog owned by a white couple who didn't care about black people and let their two dogs roam freely knowing full well they could attack and even kill black children who went by their house everyday on their way to and from school. I was one of those children, as I explained earlier, and the incident was seared in my memory.

I remember the incident as if it happened only yesterday. And it will be with me for the rest of my life, not because I want to relive it but because it became an integral part of my identity from the day it happened. And it continues to haunt me and constantly remind me who and what I am in this world, not just another human being but a black one.

That is the kind of world we live in. Even after all the years, thousands of years, we have lived together on this planet, many people still refuse to accept the fundamental fact that we are all just human more than anything else, a common bond that transcends everything else that unites and divides us as different people. That is the reality, however harsh and uncomfortable it may be to some of them.

My parents also experience racism, especially my father because he worked with whites in Tanganyika during colonial rule. He was not even allowed to eat his lunch or put it on the table in the office he shared with his white supervisor. But the white supervisor could eat there simply because he was white and believed he had absolute control over my father. He could not accept the idea that a black man had the temerity to think he was equal to whites.

I even wrote a book about those days when we lived under British colonial rule. When I was writing the book, *Life in Tanganyika in The Fifties,* I interviewed one former British settler, in 2006, who once lived in Tanganyika during the same period I did and he had this to say:

"The behaviour of the white settlers towards the Africans was not always as good as it should have been....

I remember being shocked to hear one European admit that he treated his dogs better than he treated his African staff....

Whites and Africans just did not mix. The white population had their meeting places and the Africans likewise. I was not aware of any Europeans who were opposed to the status quo....

The House servants were a vital part of everyday life; but were very firmly kept in place.

I did though, witness one distressing event. An African was walking along a town street (in Nachingwea, southern Tanganyika), minding his own business, when an Alsatian leapt at him from the back of a pick-up truck. The African was shocked and scared witless. He leapt out of the way and into the road. He landed in the path of an oncoming car.

The (white) driver of the car only just managed to pull up in time. He leapt out of his vehicle and punched the hapless African in such a way that his jaw was fractured. Dad took it upon himself to ferry the unfortunate man to the local hospital....

The Europeans had arrived and taken over the best land for themselves. There was an overwhelming feeling that the African 'so newly brought out of barbarism' was incapable of looking after himself without the benevolent eye of the European. For the most part White and African got on. Mainly this was because the African 'knew his place'....

Many Europeans were aware that not enough was being done for the welfare of the Africans, but were unwilling to say so for fear of disturbing their own newly acquired life-style. My father had signed a contract to head a school for Europeans (in Nachingwea).

He was not allowed to teach African children. The only Africans who got near the place were those learning to become office workers. They came to what was effectively nightschool....

The idea of being led by Africans was anathema to a great many Europeans...." – ((Nicholas Edmondson, UK, interviewed by Godfrey Mwakikagile, *Life in Tanganyika in The Fifties*, Third Edition, New Africa Press, 2010, pp. 258 - 259, 260 – 263, 264 - 265, 266).

The idea of being led by black people may have been

anathema to most whites but they were not going to rule us forever regardless of how superior they thought they were to us; and they did, even after independence. Some of them treated black people worse than they did dogs or put them in the same category with them and other animals.

They did not even respect our national leaders who led the struggle for independence. Julius Nyerere, who became the first prime minister and then president of Tanganyika after he led the country to independence from Britain, was one such victim. He was subjected to indignities of colour bar in the same ordinary black Tanganyikans were. As I state in one of my books, *Nyerere and Africa: End of an Era*:

"Mwalimu [Julius Nyerere] himself had experienced racial discrimination, what we in East Africa – and elsewhere including southern Africa – also call colour bar. As Colin Legum states in a book he edited with Tanzanian professor, Geoffrey Mmari, *Mwalimu: The Influence of Nyerere*:

I was privileged to meet Nyerere while he was still a young teacher in short trousers at the very beginning of his political career, and to engage in private conversations with him since the early 1950s.

My very first encounter in 1953 taught me something about his calm authority in the face of racism in colonial Tanganyika. I had arranged a meeting with four leaders of the nascent nationalist movement at the Old Africa Hotel in Dar es Salaam. We sat at a table on the pavement and ordered five beers, but before we could lift our glasses an African waiter rushed up and whipped away all the glasses except mine.

I rose to protest to the white manager, but Nyerere restrained me. 'I am glad it happened,' he said, 'now you can go and tell your friend Sir Edward Twining [the colonial governor at the time] how things are in this country.'

His manner was light and amusing, with no hint of anger.

Simple, yet profound. For, beneath the surface lay a steely character with a deep passion for justice across the colour line and an uncompromising commitment to the egalitarian ideals he espoused and implemented throughout his political career, favouring none.

Years later his son, Andrew Nyerere, told me about an incident that also took place in the capital Dar es Salaam shortly after Tanganyika won independence in 1961 near the school he and I attended and where we also stayed from 1969 – 1970. Like the incident earlier when Julius Nyerere was humiliated at the Old Africa Hotel back in 1953, this one also involved race. As Andrew stated in a letter to me in 2002 when I was writing this book:

As you remember, Sheikh Amri Abeid was the first mayor of Dar es Salaam. Soon after independence, the mayor went to Palm Beach Hotel (near our high school, Tambaza, on United Nations Road in Upanga). There was a sign at the hotel which clearly stated: 'No Africans and dogs allowed inside.' He was blocked from entering the hotel, and said in protest, 'But I am the Mayor.' Still he was told, 'You will not get in.' Shortly thereafter, the owner of the hotel was given 48 hours to leave the country. When the nationalization exercise began, that hotel was the first to be nationalized.

Such insults were the last thing that could be tolerated in newly independent Tanganyika. And President Nyerere, probably more than any other African leader, would not have tolerated, and did not tolerate, seeing even the humblest of peasants being insulted and humiliated by anyone including fellow countrymen." – (Godfrey Mwakikagile, *Nyerere and Africa: End of an Era*, Fifth Edition, New Africa Press, 2010, pp. 501 – 502).

There was also residential segregation in urban areas reminiscent of apartheid South Africa and the United States during and even after the era of segregation. Members of different races lived in their own areas. Dar es Salaam was a typical example. As Trevor Grundy, a British journalist who worked in Tanzania at the same newspaper where I also worked as a news reporter during the same period, stated in his review of Professor Thomas Molony's book, *Nyerere –The Early Years*:

"The British turned Tanganyika into an undeclared apartheid state that was socially divided between divided Africans, Europeans and Asians....It was British-style apartheid – their secret was never to give racial segregation a name." – (Trevor Grundy, "Julius Nyerere Reconsidered," review of Thomas Molony, *Nyerere – The Early Years*, africaunauthorised.com, 4 May 2015).

The years I spent under segregation when I was growing up in different parts of Tanganyika shaped my thinking and perspective on race relations and on the impact of colonial rule on the colonised when I became a writer of non-fiction books about colonial and post-colonial Africa.

There was also racial discrimination in employment during colonial rule when I was growing up in the fifties. Europeans, Asians and members of other races earned more than Africans did even if they had the same skills and level of education. My father was a victim of such discrimination when he worked for the colonial government.

So, there are many similarities between colonial Tanganyika – as well other African countries ruled by Europeans – and the United States in terms of how black people were treated and are still treated by many whites and members of other races.

I am a product of that experience under British colonial rule. It was racial injustice. I have also witnessed and experienced racism in the United States.

Black people are perceived the same way by many whites regardless of where they live.

Millions of whites, not just in the United States but round the globe, still don't believe black people are equal to them; so do many other nonblacks who also think they are better than blacks simply because they are not black although they themselves were also conquered and ruled by whites and are still controlled by them in many ways.

We are the most despised people on Earth, and the most humiliated.

It all started with the conquest of Africa by Europeans. The imperial logic was that conquered people were not equal to their conquerors in any conceivable way.

We have been objects of ridicule and contempt since then.

Contempt for black people, and black lives, has been an integral part of the black experience for centuries not only in Africa but also in the diaspora.

It was tragically demonstrated in the United States in contemporary times when the country veered off its course under President Donald Trump who was an embodiment of white supremacy and relished his role in dividing the nation along racial lines.

And he succeeded in doing so, with dire consequences for the country and its future; black people being some of the primary victims as prime targets of racial injustices more than anybody else.

The election of Trump as president of the United States legitimised white supremacy among tens of millions of whites who voted for him and even among many others who did not but who agreed with him on matters of race. It also exposed a deep chasm between blacks and whites and the myth that the country had virtually overcome racism in most areas of life. It is a myth that has been used to justify neglect of the victims of racial injustices and it continues to be used that way.

Having lived with the race problem for more than 400 years since the founding of the nation whose very foundation was based on slavery, itself a racist institution even if its primary motivation was economic, it seems highly unlikely that the United States will ever overcome racial injustices as a nation deeply divided along racial lines. History bears witness to that. The 2020 presidential election was a warning of things yet to come. It was dire warning about the future of the country after showing how divided it is.

Contrary to great expectations among many people of all races, and even among tens of millions around the world just like in the United States, the American presidential election on 3 November 2020 was *not* a repudiation of Trump and Trumpism – his toxic views and policies and so on. It was only partial repudiation but mainly a vindication of Trump and Trumpism, especially his racist beliefs, by almost half of the country.

That is why he won more than 74 million votes, an impressive feat constituting about half of the entire electorate in a country that has supposedly conquered racism in most areas. It was also the largest number of votes ever won by a Republican presidential candidate in the nation's history.

Therefore, Trump also won in some respects in the 2020 presidential election that was highly toxic and which will be remembered for its toxicity probably more than any other in modern American history because of his racism and xenophobia against blacks and other nonwhites, among other things, including his incendiary rhetoric on many subjects.

Joe Biden won almost 81 million votes, the largest number ever garnered by a candidate in an American presidential election.

Yet Trump, more than Biden, will remain a potent force in American politics and national life for a long time even after he dies, serving as a lightning rod when his supporters invoke his name and legacy to galvanise his base and get even more support from other people in different parts of the country in future elections which will still be partly determined by almost half of the entire electorate he won in the 2020 presidential election.

If he does not win the presidential Republican primary

in 2024 to become the party's nominee, his clone will. And there will be many who would like to be like him because of the enormous influence he wields in the Republican party and beyond.

Even if none of them emerges to be the standard flag bearer of the Republican party in the 2024 election, and a traditional Republican instead clinches the nomination, the impact Trump has had on the party, and the damage he has caused, will last for many years, affecting the party's fortunes in future elections.

After losing the election to Biden, he became a spent force, but not his influence, especially in the Republican party. Hated as much as he is loved, he has made history in a way no other American president or national political figure has, as the nation awaits the verdict of history on his presidency. It is a verdict that may not be kind to him more than any other American president.

But there is no question that he inspired tens of millions of people beyond his base of core supporters and they gravitated towards him in a way political pundits did not expect, defying polls and expectations of some of the most seasoned observers across the ideological spectrum. White nationalism played a major role in winning him massive support among tens of millions of whites.

White conservatives and others have sought political and ideological sustenance from white nationalist hysteria to pursue their agenda and it works. It is a lethal weapon against blacks and other nonwhites who are considered to be less American than whites.

The mere fact that Trump was not only able to galvanise half of the country into supporting his candidacy – hence his policies and racist agenda – but was actually embraced by tens of millions of voters, mostly white, in spite of his blatantly racist views should be more than enough to send a shudder down the spine of every man and woman of conscience in a country that prides itself of being the land of racial equality and a beacon of hope to millions round the globe who are struggling to live their lives as normal human beings in pursuit of liberty, equality and happiness in their own countries without necessarily trying to move to America.

With all the things he said and did including breaking the law, abusing his office and the power of the presidency and making a mockery of the institutions which made America a great nation; in spite of all the insults he hurled at blacks and even women of all races, his xenophobic rage against non-white immigrants including his famous description of African countries as "shithole countries"; in spite of all that and much more including impeachment against him which was based on a mountain of evidence against him, nothing – absolutely nothing – was able to jolt the conscience of tens of millions of people – mostly white voters – into acknowledging that he was *not* the right person to lead the country. He was clearly the wrong person to lead the most powerful nation on Earth – and would have been the wrong person to lead even the weakest country had he been a citizen there.

At a very elementary level, it was clear, abundantly clear, that he flouted norms of democracy and decency, alienated allies, and pursued polices deliberately intended to subvert American institutions. Yet, to millions – tens of millions – of his supporters, he did nothing wrong, absolutely nothing, to undermine America. Even his racist rhetoric endeared him to millions of whites.

They are the other America. Yet, for all practical purposes, they are the America that has always existed as America for more than 400 years as the land for white people, keeping blacks and other nonwhites on the periphery of the mainstream.

If for more than 400 years America has failed or has simply refused to accept black people as equal citizens entitled to the same rights white people are, and enjoying – in the practical sense – the same rights whites do, there is no reason why one should believe it will do so in the future.

There are grounds for such scepticism even in contemporary times in a country where only four years ago in 2016, a man who openly campaigned from a racist platform and was endorsed and supported by white spremacists won the presidential election and almost won again in 2020.

He did not hide his racist views. He did not mute his racist rhetoric. The tens of millions of people who voted for him, most of them white, heard what he said about blacks and other nonwhites – and *still* voted for him to be president of the Untied States.

And there is no reason to believe another candidate with similar views, racist and xenophobic, is not going to win the presidential election, supported and voted into office by tens of millions of whites who couldn't care less if black people and other nonwhites were permanently denied equal rights. Otherwise they wouldn't support and vote for a racist to be president. As Malcolm X once said: "The same problem we had a hundred years ago is the same problem we are going to have a hundred years from now." And as Margaret Renki stated in her article, "71 Million People Voted for Trump. They're Not Going Anywhere. We are Still a Painfully Divided Nation," in *The New York Times*, 9 November 2020, six days after the presidential election:

"For at least a week before Election Day, I was too anxious to focus. Donald Trump was running a re-election campaign founded in lies, and I had no faith that my fellow Americans would throw him out. The polls were reassuring, but I wasn't reassured. Polls were reassuring in 2016, too, and this country still ended up in an abusive relationship with the most corrupt and dangerous president of my lifetime.

I had no faith, but I held out hope. The ubiquity of the anti-Trump ads created by The Lincoln Project, a group of

Republican operatives endorsing Joe Biden, gave me hope. A change of heart in so many of my conservative friends — disgusted by Mr. Trump's greed and deception and boorish behavior, disgusted by his inexplicable subservience to foreign despots, his encouragement of outrageous conspiracy theories, his loyalty to his own interests and no one else's — gave me hope. Above all, the massive registration and get-out-the-vote effort in Black communities across the country gave me hope. Change was in the air — I could feel it. An uprising was upon us. A great repudiation was at hand....

People have had four years now to find out just how truly terrible Mr. Trump is. How indifferent he is to the norms of civil discourse and to the responsibilities of democracy itself. How transparently racist he is, how divisive, how selfish. We know he's a chronic liar who, when caught out, simply doubles down on the lie. We know that he is using the levers of government to enrich himself. We know he delights in and urges on the most violent impulses of his most dangerous followers. We know he has let 237,000 Americans die on his watch and still has no plan for saving the rest of us (from the coronavirus pandemic).

The numbers as of Sunday revealed that more than 71 million people voted for him anyway — *eight million more* than voted for him in 2016....

The 71 million people who voted for Donald Trump despite his incompetence, despite his lying, his bullying, his cheating, his racism, despite all the moral failings he proudly flaunts as virtues? Those people aren't going anywhere, the poison-spewing right-wing media that created them isn't going anywhere, and Donald Trump himself isn't going anywhere. And it's not remotely clear what the rest of us can do about any of that."

Why did so many people, tens of millions, vote for Trump? They voted for him because they believed he was right *and* had the right to be racist as much as they do or at least as much as almost half of the entire country does. And therein lies the tragedy of America: its inability or unwillingness to acknowledge – the unwillingness of at least half of the electorate – its moral failure on matters of race and its refusal to do something about it. That is *why* it refused to repudiate Trump.

Trump's racial views prevailed and almost catapulted him to victory in the 2020 presidential election, and could have, had there been no massive voter registration and turnout during the election by Democrats, including an unprecedented number of black voters who have always been the most loyal supporters of Democratic presidential candidates.

Race has always shaped American life since the founding of the nation whose primary foundation was racism and racial inequalities. During Trump's presidency, contempt for blacks became a mobilisjng tool for his supporters, a phenomenon – denigration of an entire people – that has been an integral part of American history, in spite of the fact that the people who are despised so much are the very ones who built this country for centuries without being paid a penny.

Fortunately, not all whites feel that way. But even today, black people are routinely despised by many whites and by many people of other races just like their brethren in Africa are; so are the rest of blacks round the globe where it is hard for black people to get respect.

It is a contempt that seems to have no end.

www.ingramcontent.com/pod-product-compliance
Lightning Source LLC
Chambersburg PA
CBHW031111250726
48655CB00004B/1670